THRESHOLD

Professor Alexander Batthyány, PhD, is director of the Research Institute for Theoretical Psychology and Personalist Studies at Pázmány Péter Catholic University in Budapest, professor for existential psychotherapy at the Moscow Institute of Psychoanalysis, and director of the Viktor Frankl Institute of Logotherapy in Vienna. He is the author or editor of more than fifteen books, and his academic work has been translated into ten languages. He has also been invited to give lectures around the world. Batthyány divides his time between Vienna and the Hungarian countryside.

THRESHOLD

TERMINAL LUCIDITY AND THE BORDER BETWEEN LIFE AND DEATH

ALEXANDER BATTHYÁNY

SCRIBE

Melbourne | London | Minneapolis

Scribe Publications
18–20 Edward St, Brunswick, Victoria 3056, Australia
2 John Street, Clerkenwell, London WC1N 2ES, United Kingdom
3754 Pleasant Ave, Suite 100, Minneapolis, Minnesota 55409, USA

First published in the United States by St. Martin's Essentials,
an imprint of St. Martin's Publishing Group 2023

Published in Australia and New Zealand by Scribe 2023
Published in the UK by Scribe 2024

Printed and bound in the UK by CPI Group (UK) Ltd, Croydon CR0 4YY

Scribe Publications is committed to the sustainable use of natural resources
and the use of paper products made responsibly from those resources.

978 1 761380 80 8 (Australian edition)
978 1 915590 66 4 (UK edition)
978 1 761385 43 8 (ebook)

Catalogue records for this book are available from the
National Library of Australia and the British Library.

scribepublications.com.au
scribepublications.co.uk
scribepublications.com

To Juliane, Leonie, and Larissa
and the memory of Sir John C. Eccles

—Vienna and Sitke, January 2023

Contents

Part II. Terminal Lucidity

PART I

On Being Someone

We who must die demand a miracle.
—W. H. Auden

On Being Someone, and Yet to Die

A Look Behind the Obvious

According to a proverb, when a person dies, a world dies. Someone has *been here*—had a sense of self, held hopes, desires, and ideals, struggled, succeeded, loved, was loved—all the things, in other words, that constitute the discrete dignity of a human life. Both spectacular and common; ordinary yet extraordinary.

Now change the scene. Today, this person lies on his deathbed. His breathing slows down, his pulse weakens, his heartbeats become irregular. And then, the last breath. There will be no tomorrow for this person, there will be no next week, there will be no next month. A life has come to its end; a private world has shut down forever. But is this person and his or her world, as the proverb suggests, gone forever? Is it all irretrievably lost? And is that it? I will discuss these questions, and many others, in the course of this book.

This book tells the story of my present research work on consciousness, cognition, dementia, and death and dying. In this book, I will share personal stories and testimonies from people who witnessed some remarkable phenomena pertinent to these questions, many who contacted me after my interest in certain death bed phenomena was reported by several media outlets. They told me stories about loved ones who are long gone now; stories about those whose way of dying was often profoundly moving and beautiful—but scientifically puzzling.

And puzzling it is. For the majority of these people were severely impaired before they died; most suffered from dementia or similarly devastating neurological disorders. They were confused, had forgotten most details about their earlier lives, and some of them didn't even know their own names. Due to progressive brain diseases, they had lost their private worlds, perhaps even their self-identity, long before they died. Given their diagnosis and years of mental and cognitive decline, one might not expect their stories to be inspiring and reassuring. But why, then, did most of those who witnessed the deaths of these persons describe the experience as "beautiful," as a "gift," and as an assurance, if not tangible evidence, that there is something about our personhood—our core self—that is whole, safe, sheltered, sound, and protected even in the face of illness and frailty, even in the face of death? And why did many insist that after what they had witnessed, their conviction grew that life is meaningful—that we, *our* lives, are meaningful; so meaningful, in fact, that nature or existence, if you will, seems to have bestowed us with a self that is in some fundamental ways preserved and protected even when all that outside observers can see is decline, dementia, and finally, death?

The answer is that their deaths were extraordinary because they experienced a phenomenon which has recently been termed "terminal lucidity," or "lightening up before death." Terminal lucidity is the technical term for the unexpected return of cognitive clarity, self-awareness, memory, and lucid functioning of patients who were assumed to have permanently lost their mental capacities.[1] We observe (and study) this phenomenon in people with severe dementia or Alzheimer's disease, as well as in people who have suffered strokes and other massive health crises, people who have been unconscious and/or unresponsive for long periods, and people who have been incapacitated by severe and chronic mental illness. Many, in fact most, had been given up on by their doctors and their relatives and friends—the dementias and other chronic neurological disorders are mostly held to be irreversible. Spontaneous healing, or a "return of the old, premorbid self" is not to be expected; it is not in the textbooks. And yet, at the hour of their death, some of these patients make what my friend and colleague, near-death research pioneer and professor of psychology Kenneth Ring calls "a miraculous return."[2]

The phenomenon as such is not new. But for a long time, it didn't even have a name. And for most of that time, there were no attempts to study and understand, even to acknowledge it. Reports of this phenomenon are scattered in the older medical literature, but it was long seen as a mere medical curiosity: one of those clinical observations that, while being occasionally noted down in medical reports, was deemed too rare to warrant scientific attention. Every researcher, and most clinicians know that occasionally things happen that are unexpected, unlikely, or simply strange. They happen, and they are either written off as weird (if sometimes overwhelmingly beautiful) onetime events, or they are forgotten—or they become anecdotes. Perhaps you talk about them in the breaks of research meetings of conferences, or over lunch with a colleague, or you share them with your spouse or your friends. But you rarely present them as your main findings during your lectures, nor would you write scientific papers about them. And if you did write and submit a paper for publication, passing peer review would be unlikely.

Sometimes, however, these events make you pause and wonder, and when you wonder long enough, it won't be possible to simply continue ignoring them. And when you begin to take them seriously, they might impact a whole research career. They did mine, as you will see in the course of this book. For my colleague (and my co-author of one of the first studies on contemporary terminal lucidity cases), professor of psychiatry and near-death research pioneer Bruce Greyson, it was the encounter with a patient who "saw" a spaghetti stain on Bruce's tie that had such an impact. Not because of the stain, but because the patient "saw" it while being on what she claimed to be an extensive excursion out of her body. To the attending physicians (Bruce among them), she seemed unconscious and unresponsive. She actually was lying on an emergency bed in the ICU of her local hospital, knocked out by a vast overdose of sleeping medication. It was this spaghetti stain that started Bruce's lifelong research into near-death experiences: "For the past half century, I've been trying to understand how Holly could have known about that spaghetti stain," he writes in his autobiography.[3]

Yet for the most part, such onetime experiences remain just that. It is only when accounts of such events reach a critical mass and are reported with increasing frequency that you begin to see a pattern and it slowly dawns on you that you can no longer intellectually afford to ignore them. Only then might they attract the scientific interest of more researchers. And indeed, only recently did researchers—among them Michael Nahm[4] in Freiburg, Sandy Macleod at the Nurse Maude Hospice in Christchurch, New Zealand, Joan M. Griffin's international research group at the Kern Center (Mayo Clinic, Rochester), and my research groups both at University of Vienna and at Pázmány University in Budapest—begin to systematically study cases of terminal lucidity in more detail.

For the past ten years or so, I have tried to better understand what terminal lucidity is all about and have collected a large database of case reports, a file that is still growing. And yet, terminal lucidity—each single case, in fact—remains an enigma, not least because it (like the near-death experience) touches upon some intimate and existential, even spiritual questions about the nature of the self and how the self may or may not persist throughout a life's journey including times of illness, impairment, and finally, death. Hence the following is but a first chapter of a longer story of what is yet to come; but it is a story already worth being told—and, perhaps even more important, it contains many individual stories worth being heard.

Stories and Data: Finding Light in Unlikely Places

To give you an initial idea of what will follow in later chapters, let me illustrate this tension between sober research work and the personal, existential aspects of this work. It is one thing to write in your case report that an eighty-six-year-old female patient with advanced Alzheimer's experienced terminal lucidity. In a table, that's precisely four data points: age, sex, diagnosis, unexpected event (terminal lucidity). It is yet another thing to read the family members' personal account of what actually happened when this patient died:

> My grandmother had suffered from Alzheimer's dementia for several years. Putting her under the care of a nursing home was a difficult decision for all of us, especially for the man of her life, whom she'd been married to for more than sixty years—but at some point, looking after her at home simply exceeded the strength of this old man, who was devoted to his wife. In the final stages of her illness, nothing much seemed to remain of the grandmother I knew and loved. At first, she could no longer recognize us. Eventually, she stopped speaking altogether and had to be fed, because she was no longer capable of eating unaided. My grandfather nonetheless called on her every day: one visit in the morning and one in the afternoon. Our family went to see my grandmother every

Sunday. Truth be told, we didn't so much visit my grandmother as support my grandfather those Sundays. On the day "the miracle" happened, we reached the door, knocked, entered the room—and saw how my grandfather lovingly held my grandmother's hand and, yes, spoke to her! At first, we just didn't trust our eyes and ears. But then my grandmother looked at us one by one (all five of us). Her large, beautiful eyes were perfectly clear. The haze of oblivion, of apathy, the "dead gaze" had given way to an expression of limpid vitality. Like bright water. I cannot think of a better image. She who hadn't recognized us for a year, who hadn't even reacted when we visited her, addressed every one of us by name. She who'd removed her hand when we wanted to take it, presumably on reflex. On that day, however, my grandmother said in plain, clear German that she was glad to "be back," and to see us.

Then she looked lovingly at her husband, my grandfather, and asked us to take good care of him. She said it was no good him being alone in the big house (my grandfather then lived in the large house that was my mother's childhood home) and that he needed domestic help. When we said that he had recently hired a housekeeper, she simply said: "Yes, but you could have told me!" (We hadn't done so, because talking to, let alone with, her only a day prior would have been unthinkable.) However, now she clearly understood and was reassured. She took his hand. I saw my grandfather's face—thick tears were running down his cheeks. Between sobs, he barely managed to say: "I love you." And she answered: "I love you!" And her gaze . . . I myself weep as I write this down, because I can see the clarity, urgency, and love her eyes expressed that day as clearly as if I could see them now.

This conversation lasted some twenty or thirty minutes. Then my grandmother lay back and soon fell asleep. We stayed at her bedside for another half hour or so, until the end of visiting time. None of us talked when we left. My grandfather linked arms with me as we walked out, but he tore away from me after a few meters and turned back in the corridor of the nursing home, because he wanted to kiss his wife once more. It was to be for the last time. When the phone rang the next morning, I knew before picking up what the ward nurse was going to tell us. My grandmother had died peacefully in her sleep, at the age of eighty-six. It was one of the most beautiful and wondrous and moving things I have witnessed to this day.

This case carries no. CH34 (i.e., Swiss case no. 34) in my database; the case description came as an accompaniment/appendix of a standardized questionnaire I sent out to several hundred caretakers and family members of recently deceased, neurologically impaired patients. The data of case CH34 went into a larger database of contemporary cases of a study on terminal lucidity that I conducted, and were finally published in 2019 with co-author Bruce Greyson. Some of these, and additional findings, will be presented later in this book. But as we just saw, there is so much more to this experience. So much more, in fact, than a researcher can publish in his or her research papers or reports. What about the story and the lived experience behind the data of CH34, or, for that matter, the stories behind the many other cases? The granddaughter who sent me this report added a brief personal note: "I thought I would let you know what *really* happened. The questionnaire items wouldn't have done justice to what we saw on that day, not even a bit."

When I started my research work into terminal lucidity, a number of respondents said or wrote something along these lines—so many, in fact, that it soon dawned on me that our early, primarily data-driven approach largely missed out on what had "really happened." A few months after I conducted my pilot studies on terminal lucidity, I therefore began to actively invite our participants to send me their stories, too; I wanted to acknowledge and appreciate what they had experienced— and I wanted to offer them a space to share what they saw, heard, and felt, especially after some of our study participants mentioned that they had sorely missed such a space in their immediate environs.

A large part of this book is about these stories and what they (and of course the actual data) can tell us about who we are—in life and in death. In the following, I will try to equally honor both approaches to the subject: the personal, and the data. Both cover areas the other cannot; both complement each other. And as we shall see, the stories themselves, even more in combination with the data, appear to tell us an exceptionally beautiful story about some forgotten aspects of human nature, and about the soul, about dignity, compassion, connection, meaning, about ourselves.

So this book is not only about stories of those who are long gone now, it is also about what we can learn from researching the no-man's-land of mind and self at the end of life. For the further we dive into this young research field and the stories behind it, the clearer it becomes that the materials we are collecting carry an important message about where we belong, what and who we are, and finally, about what we can hope for. Later on, I will also present and discuss some complementary research findings and stories on related phenomena from near-death research, and we will look at the implications these findings have for our understanding of the self, its fate in disease, and death and dying. Different stories, different data, different approaches. Yet they all point in the same direction.

To foreshadow some of the lessons I learned during this work, I will report on findings that I believe provide strong reasons for a well-founded affirmation of the unconditional meaningfulness and significance of each human life—and death. In this book, I attempt to present some of our observations in an accessible and nontechnical jargon. I believe that our work offers a message sorely needed in our times, and especially these days. Our research work into terminal lucidity strengthens the case for an outlook on life that is based on meaning, compassion, consolation, mutual acceptance and support, love, the will to heal a very broken world, and—yes: a hope that is so firm and so well-reasoned that it is in many ways stronger even than disease and death. Of course, it is an unfinished, unfolding story. But as we'll see in this book, it is very possible that *all* our stories within one single lifespan are unfinished, unfolding stories, reaching far beyond what we can currently fully grasp, or perhaps even imagine.

Life Stories, Life Meanings, Life Endings

Listening well to people as they share their observations and experiences of the deaths of their loved ones gives you a deep sense of connection. You tap into a dimension that only a person-to-person encounter can reach. People are willing to share (parts of) their lives with you, and as they share their memories, you listen. You nod. And somehow, you understand. There is a certain understanding—not a knowing, but an understanding—that happens when we carefully listen to or read these stories, these memories, of others. And you wonder: What are these memories? And frequently, in the cases of those afflicted by dementia and other severe illness discussed later in this book, you also wonder: Where are these memories now?

But most of us will die in the knowledge of who we are, what we have lived through, hoped, loved, suffered, gained, and achieved. We become older, richer in experience. It is worth telling these stories, and it is worth listening to them. Each is the testimony of a life only one person can relay—the one who lived it. In a very concrete sense, each of our lives is a chapter in the unwritten chronicles of humanity's history, and each therefore adds some element and aspect of understanding to who and what we are. As the British biologists Sir Peter B. Medawar and Jean S. Medawar put it:

> Only human beings guide their behavior by a knowledge of what happened before they were born and a preconception of what may happen after they are dead: thus only human beings find their way by a light that illumines more than the patch of ground they stand on.[5]

Both clinical research and the personal testimony of those who care for the elderly and the dying attest to this: Research as well as personal experience tell us that the days at the end of life are often days of profound understanding—of tying up loose ends, and of discovering the meaning of what one has lived through, or fulfilling that meaning until the very last breath. It is possible. It happens. I have witnessed or heard about it often enough in my own work—observations that will not go into a research or case protocol, but that perhaps will be written down in a personal diary, notes that weigh all the more on a personal, existential level. The Austrian psychiatrist Viktor Frankl once noted that he became a "real" psychiatrist only when he began to forget everything his teachers, Sigmund Freud and Alfred Adler (he had studied under both), had taught him; instead, he viewed his patients as his teachers. Others told me that they experienced something very similar; and I hope that through this book, so will you. There is so much we can learn from listening; there is so much we can gain from giving attention to those around us.

Life, Death, and Dignity

For example, experiences such as this one: A few years ago, I visited a hospice in Moscow, Russia, for a teaching assignment as visiting professor of the Moscow Institute of Psychoanalysis. We—a group of psychologists, psychotherapists, and medical doctors and students—made our round on the ward. At one point, each of us fell silent, wondering and thinking hard of what we were going to say to the patients in the double room we were about to enter. For in this double room, there were two elderly men, both in their mideighties, with end-stage pancreatic cancer. Both had lost their wives years ago, had no children, in fact had no living relatives, and most of their friends were either dead or themselves too frail to visit them. None had received a visit, a phone call, or even a postcard since they were transferred to the hospice, and we knew—and they knew—that their prognosis was bleak. Days, perhaps weeks. What, then, do you say?

Yet when we enter their room, we enter into what only can be described as a room out of the hospice, out of this world even. We see that one of them is kneeling next to the bed of the other, holding his hand, consoling him, while the other is listening gratefully and attentively. None of us "professionals" says a word. None of us can or needs to say a word. We look at each other, nod, and quietly leave the room, not sure whether the two even noticed us—but knowing that we weren't entitled to interrupt what was happening at this moment. And even now, it is hard to find appropriate words for the humaneness, dignity, and simple beauty of this encounter. But it came with three important lessons I have frequently encountered during my work, and that will also recur in this book: first, when it comes to death and dying, we need to listen and observe carefully, consciously, openly. Data are important; they inform and guide our research—but stories are perhaps even more important. They guide our lives.

Second, those at the end of life are in so many ways ahead of us. They are no longer mere patients (if anyone ever was!). Sometimes they may need support. Somebody must cook for them, or perhaps they need medical or practical help—such as taking care of their physical pain, or clothing, washing or feeding them, or perhaps they want to talk to a helping professional. Sometimes, that is. But they *always* deserve to know that we are ready to be with them, to listen to them—and not only as a mere duty, and not only with our heads, but also with our hearts. We owe it to them, and we owe it to us, and we owe it to those who will later learn from us what we have learned.

And the third lesson: it is never too late (and never too early) for meaning, compassion, love, and care; it is there, available to us and to them, until the last breath, and every breath before that, waiting to be revealed, waiting to be realized. This is true not only for those who are dying, but also for those around them: family members, friends, acquaintances, members of the helping professions, researchers. They—we—understand, see, feel that life matters when we view it through the eyes of care, support, and love.

Being a Self

In an ideal world, our life journey should begin with a childhood in the loving and caring environment of the family and end in an environment no less loving and caring. In other words, in an ideal world, we acknowledge ourselves and others as the unique persons we are—as someone, not as something, at every stage of life, in health or sickness. On a certain level—on the level of love, of a real person-to-person encounter—it does not matter what and how we are. What matters is who we are: unique and irreplaceable, in life and in death, and, as we shall see, perhaps even beyond.

To illustrate this point, let me share a story from my psychotherapy teacher. The Austrian clinical psychologist Elisabeth Lukas tells of the tragic case of two men who were identical twins; one died of heart failure, leaving behind a grieving family. But from then on, whenever the surviving twin visited his dead brother's family, his small children shied away and even hid from him. Try to imagine what they saw with their eyes (similarity) and what they felt in their hearts (this is not our father). Outwardly, it was as if their lost father had come home, but it was *not him*. No matter how much his voice and demeanor resembled those of the deceased, he still wasn't the same person. His memories and life stories were not those of their father; his self was not their father's self. Mere similarity cannot override identity, individuality. In other words: what counts is who we are as irreplaceable, individual selves. And what holds true here holds true for every human person, including those who are frail, and even those who can no longer communicate or are unconscious. Every sign of life emanating from us is deeply personal, imbued with our personhood, and thus is incomparable and unique. Being a person isn't so much what we do, or how we outwardly appear, as it is what we are. Sir Charles S. Sherrington, one of the pioneers of modern neurophysiology who, jointly with Edgar Adrian, received the 1932 Nobel Prize in Physiology for his groundbreaking work on the functions of neurons, described these characteristics and the essence of this self in almost poetic terms:

> Each waking day is a stage dominated for good or ill, in comedy, farce, or tragedy, by a "dramatis persona," the "self." And so it will be until the curtain drops. This self is a unity. The continuity of its presence in time, sometimes hardly broken by sleep, its inalienable "interiority" in (sensual) space, its consistency of viewpoint, the privacy of its experience, combine to give it status as a unique existence. . . .

It regards itself as one, others treat it as one. It is addressed as
one, by a name to which it answers. The Law and the State
schedule it as one.[6]

The biography of this self—our story—thus "belongs" to us in a
unique and concrete sense—which is but one reason why it is worth
listening to it. It helps us understand who we are, and who we have
become. It helps us understand ourselves and others, and it is a testimony of our humaneness that we appreciate the story, the memories,
the life of each individual self we encounter.

2

Death, Disease, and the Question of Who We Are

Dementia and the Self

Many of us, however, also know of cases—within our own circle of friends and family, or from the accounts of others—where individuals are robbed of their memories and access to their own life stories. It is a merciless and relentless process, caused by dementia and other neurological conditions that slowly or suddenly take away memory, mental capacity, the ability to communicate, and, in very advanced states, even more than that.

Sadly, these are commonplace occurrences: the neighbor who throughout her life was a paragon of benevolence and amiability may, in the course of dementia, turn into an unhinged, irascible, and aggressive person. The art historian who, only a few years ago, wrote widely acclaimed books on Italian Renaissance paintings, has forgotten all he ever knew about the topic as a result of a rapidly growing brain tumor, and will soon cease to recognize his own wife and children. The grandmother and mother who, after a life lived for the family, supporting it with her loving warmth and care, gradually loses interest in her children and grandchildren as her dementia progresses; she will soon fail to recall their names and eventually forget that she has any children or grandchildren at all.

Such scenarios are repeated every day, across every culture, in every nation. In the United States alone, some eight to nine million people suffer from dementia, which roughly corresponds to the population of New York City; there are some fifty million sufferers worldwide, with ten million newly diagnosed cases per year—not to mention other neurological diseases or cognitive impairments sustained in the course of brain tumors, strokes, or accidents.

These cases are tragic, but there are even more repercussions. Family members, the affected persons themselves, and their caregivers often refer to feeling isolated in the face of the personal and existential questions raised by these disorders. Caregivers often suffer a dual affliction: first of all, everyday life with and for the patient must be managed, which is often difficult and painful enough. Second, however, during the quiet hours, when they finally have time to rest and reflect, their thoughts begin to stray: "Is this how it ends? And if this is how it ends, how could any of this, and any of what happened before, have any meaning?"

Accordingly, through my work, I have had the opportunity to correspond or converse with many family members of dementia patients who tell me that their relative's illness not only affects their daily life, but calls it into question. Many of them have the impression that their last possible remaining source of comfort—their belief in the meaning of life, their belief in a soul, their religious or spiritual belief in a human destiny that is greater, larger, untouched in fact by the ravages of dementia and other such disorders—is equally obscured, shattered even, when they ponder the implications of the silent drama that is unfolding before their eyes. "How can I find consolation and comfort in the belief in something nonmaterial and spiritual if the illness shows me that these nonmaterial or spiritual dimensions may not exist at all, or that these dimensions are so fragile and utterly at the mercy of material conditions?" they ask. "How can I keep my hope if the basis of my hope is fading in front of me? How can I believe, if I can see before my own eyes that the self seems ultimately to be no more than mere biology?"

And frequently: "If that is all, what is it for? What did my grandfather live for if everything he has become in his long life, the only thing he was able to hold on to—his memories, his self, his character, his individuality—is destroyed by his illness? How can there be meaning to our individual lives under these circumstances?"

Every day, millions of family members and friends of those affected have to witness how biology (i.e., disease or brain damage) seems to erase everything that this person ever was. Millions witness how small and very subtle pathological processes in the brain of a loved one lead to the progressive loss of her private world of memories, or even the apparent loss of her very identity. They watch as the traditional markers of the self—personality, speech, memory, awareness—erode or completely vanish:

"Dad, it's me, Scotty . . . your youngest son."
I never thought I'd have to say those words—words pregnant with pain and sadness. I was still learning to accept the fact that my dad no longer recognized me. He had forgotten my face. He had forgotten my name. And this forgetting was far more difficult than I had expected. [. . .] Nothing prepared me for this new chapter in my life, learning to love and care for a father who could no longer remember his own son.[1]

Questions of Life and of Death

Dementia is frequently spoken of as a disease that leaves nothing but a debased body, a "grim reminder of the person once there." But what is left of this adult son's father, once the disease has deprived him of his private world, his memories, his identity, and—so it seems—his very personhood? What has become of his memories, his private world?

Whatever our answer to this question may be, it will have direct implications for how we define the self—and ourselves, too. So, what does all this tell us about the fate of this self and other selves, especially in death and dying? Is the personality, the self, of a dementia patient irretrievably destroyed as a result of neuropathological processes? And if the integrity of my personhood is so dependent on the integrity of my brain function, does this not also clearly imply that myself, my mind, my personality are ultimately no more than products of my brain? That any idea of the "soul" and the discussion about the possibility of a future destiny of the "soul," as suggested by religious traditions, is indeed hopelessly antiquated and naïve?

Clearly, these questions do not only concern people affected by cognitively impairing brain diseases, or their family members and friends. They also challenge much of what many of us commonly assume or believe or hope to believe about the nature of the self as being more than just a product or fiction of the wonderfully complex machinery of our brains.

Socrates in the Giver's Hand

Most spiritual and religious traditions—the very traditions that have to a great extent shaped our understanding of our place in the world—have taken for granted that each of us harbors and retains something indestructible, meaningful, eternal, and true, beyond illness and possibly even beyond death. We humans encounter both the beauty of nature and its dangers, yet somehow hope, and often believe that there is, outside of time and space, another realm that is where we come from, and where we will eventually return. Research in the history and psychology of religion suggests that this was, for a long time, an almost universally held belief in most wisdom and spiritual traditions. Translated into contemporary language, these traditions thus held that each of us, each self, is somehow sheltered from being fully at the mercy of biological forces, sickness, disease, and death, though clearly affected by them. The British explorer and Orientalist Freya Madeline Stark wrote poignantly and humbly about the aging process and how it shrinks one's world as one moves closer to death; but she also wrote about her religious hopes in the face of decline and death—her trust in what she called "the Giver's hand":

> We move there with increasing freedom as Time rubs out the illusions of possession, whose dark attendant, envy, fades away. The loss of our own things, or such we thought so, our faculties, our friends, our loves—makes us again receptive as in childhood, though now it is no human hand that gives. In our increasing poverty, the universal riches grow more apparent, the careless showering of gifts regardless of return; our private grasp lessens, and leaves us heirs to infinite loves in a common world where every joy is a part of one's personal joy. With a loosening hold returning toward acceptance, we prepare in the anteroom for a darkness where even this last personal flicker fades, and what happens will be in the Giver's hand alone.[2]

And one of the most famous and arguably most beautiful and dignified testimonies of this hope and faith comes to us from Socrates. Socrates—one of the first individuals in history known to have been

sentenced to death on account of his uncompromising wisdom—
prepares himself and his students for his death:

> "But my friends," he said, "we ought to bear in mind that, if
> the soul is immortal, we must care for it, not only in respect
> to this time, which we call life, but in respect to all time, and
> if we neglect it, the danger now appears to be terrible. For if
> death were an escape from everything, it would be a boon to
> the wicked, for when they die they would be freed from the
> body and from their wickedness together with their souls.
> But now, since the soul is seen to be immortal, it cannot
> escape from evil or be saved in any other way than by be-
> coming as good and wise as possible. For the soul takes with
> it to the other world nothing but its education and nurture,
> and these are said to benefit or injure the departed greatly
> from the very beginning of his journey thither."[3]

Thereupon Socrates begins his preparations for his own execution.
In Athens, this was carried out in the traditional manner, which required the convict to drain the "cup of hemlock," a brew made from
the sap of the poisonous hemlock, which after ingestion causes paralysis and hypothermia from the legs up. But before drinking from the
poisonous cup, Socrates first takes a bath in order to save the bereaved
the trouble of washing his corpse. Human dignity to the last.

Before he drinks, his friend Crito asks Socrates about his wishes for
his funeral. Socrates takes this opportunity to emphasize once more
that the person is not the body, but the soul, and that, consequently,
there is no reason to worry about the whereabouts of the body:

> "But how shall we bury you?" [Crito asked.]
>   "However you please," Socrates replied, "if you can catch
> me and I do not get away from you." And he laughed gently,

and looking toward us, said: "I cannot persuade Crito, my friends, that the Socrates who is now conversing and arranging the details of his argument is really I; he thinks I am the one whom he will presently see as a corpse, and he asks how to bury me. And though I have been saying at great length that after I drink the poison I shall no longer be with you, but shall go away to the joys of the blessed you know of, he seems to think that was idle talk uttered to encourage you and myself."[4]

Biology and the Self: "And What About the Soul?"

This was, by all accounts, a death both heroic and beautiful—despite the fact that Socrates' death sentence was unjust, and despite that death by hemlock is, in fact, a rather unpleasant death. As the poison moves upward from toe to head, it will lead to seizures, and finally, respiratory arrest and death. Socrates, however, after lecturing to his disciples, turns to his own future fate. He is anticipating it, and this anticipation apparently far outweighs the unpleasant death throes he knows are ahead of him: "I shall no longer be with you, but shall go away to the joys of the blessed."

Such an attitude can no longer be taken for granted in today's Western world. Generally speaking, modern man seems more akin to the doubting Crito. In the past two centuries—in the wake of the continuing scientific revolution—and especially after the decade of the brain in the 1990s, humanity radically altered our self-image and, with it, our conception of life and death. Talk of the autonomy, the reality, let alone a future destiny of the soul—in fact, any mention at all of the human soul—has become much rarer. In scientifically informed circles, such talk is often considered naïve, outdated, or downright suspicious. Rather, when we talk about minds, we no longer talk about souls. We talk about brains or biology. Biology and, most prominent, brain research have thus led us to a very different way of describing who we are. We see the effects of this new self-understanding not only in scientific publications—rather, it also permeates our everyday talk of how and why we experience, feel, think, decide. For instance, we (at least, I am somewhat ashamed to say, we professionals) tend to talk less often about sadness. Instead, we talk about depression. If you google "sadness," you'll get 1.9 million hits; but google "depression," and the figure almost doubles to 3.6 million hits. And from there on, a very normal, human sentiment becomes an increasingly material, biological concept and, in the end, nothing but a biological event: depression is popularly ascribed to serotonin imbalance. Hence sadness is depression, and depression is serotonin imbalance. But next to some forms of clinical depression, which are indeed associated with (though far more complex) chemical imbalances: Can people no longer be simply sad? Perhaps their conscience and compassion are revolting against the injustice and pain we do to each other? And what, for instance, about the pain or sadness we feel when we learn that every year, around nine million people die of hunger—twenty-four thousand each day of the year—which is more than the death toll of AIDS, malaria, and tuberculosis combined? Chemical or social and moral imbalance? Or what about bereavement? Mourning the loss of someone you love seems to be so much more than just chemical; it is a deeply human expression of your love and the uniqueness and irreplaceability of the one you are missing. And yet, to explain what we feel, think, experience, love, and long for, we are shown colorful neuroimaging pictures of brains lighting up with these mental activities:

> If you are a fan of science news, then odds are you are also intrigued by brain imaging, the technique that produces those colorful pictures of brains "lit up" with activity, showing which regions are behind which behaviors, thoughts, and

emotions. So maybe you remember these recent hits: which regions of the brain listen to angry voices, which regions are active when women grieve the breakup of a romantic relationship, activity showing the problems cocaine addicts have in responding to rewards, how social rejection increases activity in the same brain regions as physical pain, how men and women show different brain activation patterns when they think about their partner cheating on them sexually (men: regions involved in sexual and aggressive behaviors such as the amygdala and hypothalamus become more active) or emotionally, which brain regions become more active when arachnophobes think about spiders, which regions become active when you first experience intense romantic love.[5]

And what about the soul? you may ask. As we saw, this is also the question often asked by those who care for dementia and other cognitively impaired neurological patients. To them, it is not merely a theoretical or philosophical question, and neither is it a question of the words we use to describe what is going on in our minds. They *need* and they *want* to know where their beloved family member or friend has gone, will go. It is an urgent question, literally a question of the life and death of the soul. But what do we—and what does our contemporary, modern narrative or model of being human—answer?

As we just saw, ever since the scientific turn and the decline of religious and spiritual traditions in the West, the modern materialist view is that our feelings, our thoughts—mind and self—even our longing for meaning and love and compassion are merely products or functions of the brain. Of course, this view isn't only based on what the ravages of dementia and other severe neurological disorders seem to tell us about the dependency of our minds on intact brain function. It is also based on a vast repository of scientific research that shows that each and every feeling, emotion, thought, choice is accompanied by a corresponding brain event. The materialist therefore concludes that the idea of a soul also is caused by brain activity alone, and that there is no need for any additional explanation for our inner lives.

So is sadness just chemical imbalance? Is love merely brain activity? Or compassion? Our care for this world and others? Or our longing to understand who we really are, and why we are here? Our sense of or longing for meaning, warmth, hope, and love? Something seems to be missing in this scheme. Something seems to fall through the coarse net of materialism.

As Estonian-Russian philosopher Valentin Tomberg put it:

> Materialism does something with regard to the world that would be absurd with regard to a work of art, namely to explain it through the qualities—and quantities—of the materials of which it consists, instead of the style, the context, the meaning, and the intention that the work of art reveals.
>
> Wouldn't it be absurd to want to understand one of Victor Hugo's poems, for example, by chemically analyzing the ink with which it had been written and the paper on which it was written, or by counting the number of words and letters?[6]

And yet for now, science, or what in the public opinion passes as "scientific authority," tends to do just that. And in doing so, it is replacing "old metaphysics" as a source of guidance and knowledge on who we really are and what our place in nature is.[7] During my studies, I often wondered: Would a modern Socrates—were he as informed and up-to-date on current scientific thinking of our days as he was of his—still be able to say, in good conscience, that "the soul is immortal"?

It is of course possible—perhaps even likely—that Socrates would have pointed out materialism is based on a decision to take seriously and therefore measure only the material (for example, brain events) with material tools, and that it is thus only able to find material objects and relations. That the problem therefore is not in what you find, but in what you look for. If you only count the red objects in a colorful painting, your description of this picture will only describe red objects. But it would be woefully incomplete. So if you measure only one thing, it is of course wildly premature to therefore claim that only those things that you measure exist, or matter. There is indeed a certain circularity in materialism in this regard.

Or we may point out that, for instance, when it comes to the argument from the dependence of a functioning mind ("soul") on a functioning brain, the differences between conditions and causes need to be taken into account. You need a pencil to write a poem (it is a condition), but nobody would therefore claim that it follows that pencils write poems (the pencil would then be, but is not, the cause of the poem). I will briefly come back to these questions in later chapters of this book, after we have looked at some recent findings that do indeed strongly suggest that the story of the brain (and its eventual cessation of functioning) may still tell a very incomplete story about who and why we are, as well as about our future destiny.

But for the moment, given the rarely questioned hold and influence of popular materialism, modern man is now more than ever faced with the challenge of relating to and understanding himself, his nature, and also his own death. He is left to decide what his mortality should mean with regard to the conduct and narrative of his life. Given the increasing erosion of a general religious consensus about the soul and the meaning of life, this is not an easy task. Role models of felicitous living and gentle dying are—or would seem to be—sorely needed. We long for them. Yet where can we find role models like Socrates in our times? And would we, in a time when we try to "outsource" dying to special hospital units, even encounter or listen to such role models? And might the rise of materialism and the decline of our willingness to honestly and openly confront death—and even more important, to be there for and with those who are dying—be causally linked?

If so, the question of our personhood and our mortality turns out to be even more fundamental. So: Which theories and data do contemporary scientific understanding confront us with? And how can spiritual hopes and concerns keep pace with them? Can they at all?

The Enchanted Loom

Many have pondered these questions—not only philosophers, but also some of the most able and prominent exponents of the study of the human brain and the biology of our minds, such as the Australian neurophysiologist Sir John C. Eccles, who, together with Sir Alan Lloyd Hodgkin and Sir Andrew Fielding Huxley, received the Nobel Prize for his discovery of the mechanism of postsynaptic inhibition of stimulus transmission in nerve fibers. Next to his research work on brain function and processes, Eccles has pondered and published throughout his life on the question of the nature of the conscious mind and the self, culminating in the collaboration with Sir Karl Popper on the book *The Self and Its Brain* (1977),[8] a manifesto, as it were, of a modern, empirically informed version of dualism; an argument that our innermost selves are beyond mere biology; that they—we—are transcendent.

I was a student when I read this book, and Eccles soon became one of my academic role models, and so I decided to write my thesis about his work. In 1996, Eccles was ninety-three years old (he would die the next year) and had just published his last and arguably most important book, with the telling title: *How the Self Controls Its Brain*.[9]

He was kind enough to grant me an interview for my thesis, which I taped with his permission. At the end of our lengthy interview—I had asked all my questions about his recent work on probability fields and the interaction problem in dualism and thought that the interview had come to a natural end—something unexpected happened. I was about to thank him for granting me so much time when Eccles paused for a moment and in turn thanked me for my questions. But, even though I sensed that he had become increasingly tired after a lengthy conversation—his voice growing lower and soft, almost to a whisper—he continued.

He mustered the strength to say something apparently significant to him—statements that might represent the intellectual and spiritual legacy of the life of an enormously productive and intellectually rigorous neuroscience scholar. They anticipate, in an almost poetic manner, a central insight of the current work undertaken by my research group, which will be presented in the next chapters of this book:

> I should like to add that to me, only one thing remains important. It is the mystery of our conscious self. As you know, I have dedicated a large portion of my research to this self—how does it come into being? What is its future destiny? In the book I have written with Sir Karl [Popper], I express my skepticism of the idea that the self is a mere product of biological processes and brain activity. I think we simply have to acknowledge that there is a mystery, transcending any biological or materialist rationale, inherent to our existence. There are thus two improbable events that point toward something beyond the biological and represent "entry points," as it were, for the metaphysical. The first event is my birth. I found myself in this life, existing as a conscious self, with this body and brain. Is my brain the creator of the self? This notion seems increasingly improbable to me. We find individual processes in the brain, but no unitary self. The brain is, to quote my teacher at Oxford Sir Charles [Sherrington],

an enchanted loom, but without the self, there is no weaver in whose hands the threads come together.

The second event is my death. Can I really believe that the amazing gift of my conscious existence has no future? No, I cannot. This incredible mind of ours relates in mysterious ways to the brain and can experience human love and friendship, the astounding beauty of nature, the intellectual stimulation and pleasure we derive from the enjoyment and understanding of our cultural heritage. This life is a challenging adventure, whose meaning must be discovered. And it is embedded in these two events, birth and death, that— and I am more convinced than ever of this—transcend both the realm of the biological and this wonderful instrument— the brain.

When Eccles spoke of the "entry points . . . for the metaphysical," and discussed the two decisive events of our life—birth and death—he clearly didn't primarily emphasize the birth, growth, decline, and decay of the body. He emphasized the role of the self or the conscious mind, transcending both biology and the brain

However, as moving and humble as Eccles's assessment of the nature of the self is, the question remains of how this view of the self can be squared with its biological vulnerability. Its apparent dependence on the integrity of the brain remains a fundamental problem, also and especially for the dualism of mind ("soul") and brain as represented by Eccles: How can the human mind, if it really is more than a mere function of the brain, be so severely impaired by a neurological disorder and often tiny biochemical changes in the brain? How does the dualist explain, for instance, the decline of dementia, or the less spectacular but similarly persuasive case for the dependence of mind on brain, such as the following?

Mind and Materialism

Ann Klinestiver was a respectable teacher in her community in Milton, West Virginia, and, as a devout Christian, she strongly disapproved of gambling—what's more, she wasn't in the least interested in it, either. However, when she developed Parkinson's disease, she was treated with the commonly used drug Requip in order to bring her tremor under control. This medication mimics the effects of dopamine on the brain, especially with regards to movement control. However, the drug showed an unusual side effect—Ann became obsessed with, and finally addicted to, gambling:

> She started gambling as soon as the track opened, at 7 A.M., and kept playing the machines until three thirty the next morning, when the security guards kicked her out. "Then I would go back home and gamble on the internet." [. . .] After a year of addictive gambling, Ann had lost more than two hundred and fifty thousand dollars. She had exhausted her retirement savings and emptied her pension fund. [. . .] "I sold everything I could sell. [. . .] I stole quarters from my grandkids. I lost everything that mattered."[10]

When, in view of this side effect, her doctors recommended discontinuation of Requip, her tremors did return, but Ann Klinestiver almost at once lost her interest in gambling. This is no isolated case; as is often the case when we look at the effect of specific neuronal factors, there is a certain regularity to it—further strengthening the case for the neuronal basis of consciousness, mind, and personality. Studies suggest that more than one in ten patients on dopamine agonists become compulsive gamblers—until they discontinue the drug. And in this specific case, the neurological mechanism is actually well understood: dopamine not only plays a role in movement control, but is also a key component of the regulatory cycle of the reward system, thus making gambling an exceedingly exciting, and addictive, activity.

As I already have pointed out, cases such as these (neurological literature is full of them) overwhelmingly demonstrate to what extent mind and personality are driven by biology. So the question remains: Given such ample evidence for the mind's dependence on the brain, how can one reasonably—and not just as a case of wishful thinking—maintain the idea of a soul (and hope for its future), if even the smallest changes in brain activity—caused by just a few milligrams of daily medication—have such massive psychological effects?

How, then, do we reconcile this with Eccles's splendid belief in a self beyond the brain? Or with Socrates' heroic death? Socrates asserted his presence of mind and unassailable belief in the continuance of the soul to the last, even in the face of his physical decline and the progressive paralysis of his limbs caused by the poisonous hemlock. At the end, Socrates covered his face with a cloth in order to spare his students the sight of his spasming features. His executioners could take his life, but not his personal dignity, nor his soul. Catch me if you can.

If, however, Socrates' farewell to his students and this world could bear witness to an independent self—his "soul"—what do we make of those dementia cases that evolve in precisely the opposite direction? In such cases, the gradual dwindling of bodily functions is not perceived by a fully conscious mind but, on the contrary, the mind and self of a person gradually slip into the realm of oblivion, while the bodily functions continue relatively unscathed. This is precisely what we observe in dementia or other severe neurological conditions. As the Australian philosopher J. J. C. Smart put it:

> Without oxygen or under the influence of anesthetic or soporific drugs, we rapidly lose consciousness. Moreover, the

quality of consciousness can be influenced in spectacular ways by appropriate drugs or by mechanical stimulation of different areas of the brain. In the face of all the evidence accumulated by modern research in neurology, it is hard to believe that after the dissolution of the brain there could be any thought or conscious experience whatsoever.[11]

So maybe there is no weaver, after all, but only the enchanted loom; and maybe the loom isn't even enchanted, but a wonderful, complex machine. But think it through, think through the implications: a wonderful biological machine is, in the final analysis, still no more than a machine. Irreparably defective machines are simply taken out of circulation. No matter how wonderful these machines may be, once they lose function and are beyond repair, they are disposed of. Questions around human dignity also arise in this context, especially those concerning the dignity of the frail and ill person. After all, it was less than eighty years ago that the city where I am writing this, Vienna, as well as all of Austria and Germany, saw at least three hundred thousand human beings fall victim to the Nazi "euthanasia" program. What had these people done? Nothing at all. Their death sentence did not stem from anything they *did,* but from what they *were*: ill, frail, depending on the help, sympathy, and compassion of others (and don't we all, to some extent?). Their mere being was enough to deny them their right to life.

At the time, people talked of a meaningless, "unworthy life"—that those whose cognitive or psychological capacities were deemed in any way limited or impaired (or just somehow unusual and departing from the norm), had ipso facto forfeited their right to life. After all, why keep a severely dysfunctional loom if there is no weaver? Such is the cold reductionism and nihilism of dictatorship. Dictatorship is generally characterized by a lack of benevolence, patience, or compassion. And it rarely has hope for the individual: hope, say, that behind the visible illness there is still something precious, true, and worthy of protection happening in an inner world, that escapes the hard gaze of those who only look for functional capacity.

But next to the social and ethical implications, there are of course also deeply personal and spiritual implications. They concern you and me and the people we love and care for; they concern in fact everything that counts: everything humane and human and beyond.

"First You Take Away the Soul"

The Austro-American philosopher Paul Edwards illustrates these implications with the example of Mrs. D, an elderly lady of his acquaintance. Mrs. D was a wealthy woman from Virginia, a banker's widow. Edwards describes her as exceptionally elegant, benevolent, generous, cultured, and kind, and continues: "I do not know what her attitude toward paralyzed or disabled people was, but I assume that she surely had empathy with them and certainly no desire to beat them up." When Mrs. D fell ill with Alzheimer's disease and her condition progressively deteriorated, she was moved to a nursing home. She shared her room with an elderly paralyzed woman confined to a wheelchair. During the first year in the nursing home, Mrs. D remained calm (if forgetful and confused), but thereafter grew increasingly aggressive and violent: "Then she started hitting the nurses. At about the time, she could no longer recognize her daughter and she beat up the paralyzed lady on two or three occasions,"[12] which resulted in her transfer to a "special ward" for particularly challenging and violent patients.

Edwards doesn't merely cite this case in order to describe the drama of dementia. Rather, he is concerned with something altogether different, namely that adherence to the "old-fashioned dualism" (like Eccles's), which maintains that the true essence of a person is not its neurological machinery but an "immaterial soul," is no longer sustainable given what dementia and other such diseases tell us about the dependence of the mind on the brain.

Edwards draws a conclusion that is as simple as its implications are sobering: Mrs. D's pronounced behavioral changes were clearly due to her illness. A dualist might argue that her true individual identity—Mrs. D's self or, to use the older, religious term, her "soul"—was still that of the amiable, kind, and considerate Mrs. D, the person she had been before her illness. That supposition presumes that her "soul" was not actually lost, but merely inaccessible, hidden, or concealed somewhere within her. Therefore, one would have to argue that Mrs. D, somewhere in her innermost self, actually recognized her daughter, but was prevented by her illness from communicating as much; and that she really had no intention of beating the nurses, let alone her fellow patient—but was somehow compelled to do so by her disorder.

Edwards reaches a different, and seemingly compelling conclusion: Mrs. D behaved amiably, graciously, reasonably, and normally precisely as long as and because her brain functioned normally. Only in the course of the disease's progress did her behavior grow more uncharacteristic of her old self; and as the disease progressed further still, the old Mrs. D vanished entirely. Her old self—her real and pre-morbid self, if you will—was lost, died, while her body was still alive. And this, according to Edwards, implies in more general terms that *our* self, our consciousness, our individuality—in short: "we"—are ultimately no more than the product of brain activity. And this conclusion applies not just to the dementia patient Mrs. D, but also to the now lost, previously healthy Mrs. D (or you and me):

If there was a "soul," brain damage could not also damage our emotional feelings, but it does. [. . .] If memory, behavior, and emotions are all controlled by the physical brain, what is a soul for? [. . .] Modern science proves that the idea of souls is misguided. Everything is biological.[13]

"Everything is biological," and to quote the British molecular biologist and co-discoverer of the DNA double helix, Francis Crick:

You, your joys and your sorrows, your memories and your ambitions, your sense of personal identity and free will, are in fact no more than the behavior of a vast assembly of nerve cells and their associated molecules.[14]

It is easy to see that this perspective does not exist in isolation. Much more is at stake here than the nature of our selves. Indeed, all of this concerns just about everything that existentially matters to us as humans. The American evolutionary biologist and historian of science William Provine has summarized the philosophical and existential implications of the "end of the soul":

It is really that simple. First, you take away the soul. You have to. There is no place for souls in science. Now once you've done away with the soul, off goes free will and the hope for an afterlife.

With these two gone, the rest follows fairly easily: there is no ultimate foundation for ethics, and there is no grand meaning of life. There are no gods or other purposive forces in the universe. You are born, you live, and you die. You are gone. When I die, I am absolutely certain that I am going to be dead. That's the end for me. There is absolutely no hope for any ultimate meaning, but there is nothing to regret about it. Not for a moment.[15]

And the British psychologist Louie Savva published another, more personal, account of the philosophical implications of this view (materialism) in an open letter to fellow psychologist (and fellow materialist) Susan Blackmore. This letter is basically a lamentation about the nihilism that accompanies uncompromising materialism:

> Consciousness is given to us by brain functioning. We are all an end product and [...] I do not think I make a difference in the universe [...]. There are three facts that I now choose to acknowledge as the most important. There is no point to life. There is no survival after death. One day, the whole universe will die. With that knowledge I now find my life almost joyless. What is the point of knowledge acquisition? Since one day it will be gone. What is the point of acquiring money to buy pointless things that I have no interest in?[16]

Certainly, this is a sobering assessment of human nature and our place in the world. It stands in stark contrast to Socrates' view of life and death, it stands in stark contrast to Eccles's view of human nature, and it denies much of what many of us believe really counts in life: meaning, love, compassion, sacredness, connection, depth.

If one wants to meet this challenge in an intellectually honest manner, it would be a fallacy to merely highlight the exceptional severity of the dementia symptoms in order to circumvent Edwards's conclusions. For Edwards's point is not that the diseased brain brought forth the untypical behavior of Mrs. D—the point rather is that the typical behavior of Mrs. D was therefore brought forth by her healthy brain, too. Additionally, the catalog of neurological disorders is replete with more selective and small malfunctions and disturbances in brain function that, while causing much less functional deterioration, nevertheless have fundamental and often dramatic effects on the conscious self and its experience and behavior.

These physiological changes often seem so insignificant that they only appear at closest inspection or under the microscope. So they might be small—tiny, in fact; but their consequences on cognitive functioning, memory, and self-identity are often bigger than life. And so are, as we have seen, their potential larger implications for the nature of personhood and our place and role in the world.

Seeing What the Eye Can't See

It is exactly for this reason that Edwards's case example of Mrs. D exerts a particularly strong intuitive argument for biological reductionism; and for the same reason, caregivers, friends, and family members of those affected by dementia frequently experience crises of their own existential meaning. Because in dementia, there seems to be no awakening, no return of the self from the respective altered or diminished state of consciousness. Intoxication, or an otherwise induced exceptional psychological state, poses a weaker challenge to the notion of an independent self, simply because these states are temporary and are followed by a return of the "old self." Just wait long enough and the same person resurfaces again. In such cases, the impaired person wasn't actually lost or destroyed, but his mind was temporarily altered under the influence of certain physiological factors. We do not question identity, nor our nature or our future beyond death in such cases—on the contrary, the smooth return of the "normal person" after such altered states should speak *for* rather than *against* a permanent personal identity. For in order to "return," it must have been "there" all the while—at least potentially, yet momentarily hidden.

As Paul Edwards's example shows, it is precisely this evidential experience of a return to normality that is missing in cases of dementia and other irreversible neurological conditions. As the illness is considered to be irreversible, and will sooner or later end in the patient's death, the idea that he (his "old self") is somehow still preserved and merely hidden behind the illness may be a pious hope, but, considering the actual circumstances, it simply isn't plausible.

But as long as it is hidden—what can we, what will we do? The thinkers and writers of the Catholic tradition of European pastoral medicine of the early twentieth century held that the naked eye missed most of what really defines a person anyway. Only the eye of charity, of love and affection, this tradition said, is able to reveal the unseen aspects of the human being: her person, her self, her hopes, what she has courageously lived through and achieved—as well as her private world. That same eye also sees what was initially planted as hope and promise within that person, but can no longer come to light, or not as clearly, as a result of illness or disability. Unless, that is, such promise is seen through the eye of affection. Once seen, care and benevolence stream forth on their own. It seems hard to imagine that these thoughts were written down only a few decades before mass killing was to beset Europe, and many of those who had written in favor of the protection of the frail and ill themselves ended up in the Dachau concentration camp, most of them in the so-called "priest blocks" (nearly 2,700 of them), reserved for priests who, among other things, would not buy into the idea of "euthanasia" and its underlying reduction of the value of a person to its mere biological functionality.

Dostoevsky once wrote that to love someone means to see him as God intended him to be. The wording may seem a little outdated to some of today's readers. Yet those who have visited some of the better-led hospice or palliative care units, and have seen with how much affection and dedication and dignity the nurses treat those under their care, *know* that these aren't merely beautiful words, but that they describe the daily reality—the everyday service—of caregivers. They have seen it with their own eyes. They have seen, through the eyes of benevolence, charity, and devotion, what is whole, sane, human, indestructible in an ill person, even if it is obscured by the symptoms of disease and disorder.

But love is based on hope, not on empirical facts. So for the researcher, or the scientifically informed thinker, that won't suffice to meet the challenge of dementia and personhood. And yet, as we will see, not only love can at times catch a glimpse of the full inner person, even if that inner person is literally hidden to the naked eye due to disease. Rather, it seems as if the other significant moment of human existence—death—does in some cases render the invisible visible—and not only to the loving glance, but in fact to *everyone* present.

3

The Return of the Self

"And Then, Something Unexpected Happened"

With this, we return to Edwards's Mrs. D and how her story might unfold. Fast forward a year or so. As a result of her further cognitive decline and aggressive behavior, she has been moved to the special ward for "problematic" cases. In this year, her mental and physical state has further deteriorated. She is only a shadow of her former self. And for the past week, she has experienced a steep physical decline. Her doctors agree that her death is imminent—a few days perhaps, maybe hours. As is customary in such cases, they inform her family—and her family members come and gather around her. They are aware of the fact that due to her advanced dementia, Mrs. D will not recognize any of them. Yet they don't come and gather around her to be recognized. They come to pay her last respects, and to say farewell to their grandmother, mother, aunt with whom they shared so many wonderful days—until her mental decline could no longer be ignored and she had to be moved to the hospital and then, the nursing home.

And yet, as they gather around her, something utterly unexpected happens. For lack of a better description, Mrs. D is "back." Life has returned to her glance; she looks like someone who has awakened from a long, long sleep. Slowly, that twinkle in her eyes returns, and so she greets each of her family members by name, smiling softly. She talks with them; her voice is low and weak, breathing is difficult. But she talks with them, to them, reminisces with them. And she bids them farewell. In brief: she "reappears" as the gentle individual—with all her memories, her private world and characteristics intact—that she had been all along *before* the onset of her illness. If only for a short period of time, the very self comes to light that Edwards declared to have been destroyed in the course of, and because of, her neurological disorder.

Her family members wonder: What does this return signify, what does it mean? How did it come about? Will she remain with us? Of all these questions, the latter one at least soon finds an answer. The very next morning, her daughter receives a phone call from the nursing home. Mrs. D has died in her sleep—in the early morning hours. But still, what happened on Mrs. D's last day? How could she regain her memories, her verbal abilities, her warmth and gentle kindness, sense of humor, her "old personality"? Her lucid episode took place *without* any noticeable change in her neurological status—her brain structure and activity, so brutally stricken by Alzheimer's, were unchanged; there is no known case in medical history in which the tissue degradation observed in Alzheimer's has ever been reversed or undone. Such a feat would come close to uncooking a boiled egg. Moreover: we now know that such cases have been observed not only in patients who, as in Mrs. D's case, were afflicted by Alzheimer's, but also in patients who had been afflicted by a myriad of other neurological illnesses. Episodes of terminal lucidity have also been reported with patients who suffered from meningitis, brain tumors or brain metastases of other primary tumors, brain abscesses and strokes, as well as chronic psychiatric disorders.[1]

As I briefly mentioned in the first chapter, such unexpected returns of the old self have been documented in individual case reports since antiquity and throughout medical history. Indeed, much of the older medical literature, particularly of the seventeenth to the early twentieth centuries, contains reports of patients who suffered from severe, incurable neurological and psychiatric disorders and whose minds were "gone" as a result—or, as Paul Edwards would say, "destroyed"—yet who unexpectedly and spontaneously recovered their memories, their sense of identity, and their "old self" at the hour of their death.

What makes these cases so remarkable is first of all their beauty, dignity, and sacredness (the words those who witness such events frequently use to describe them). And second, they are remarkable because they contradict almost everything we (or those who research the relationship between brain and mind) believe to know about the dependency of our minds on brain function ("first, you take away the soul"). When confronted with unexpected and spontaneous remissions shortly before death (terminal lucidity), one therefore cannot help but wonder what happens in such cases. Clearly, neurons do not regrow and regenerate on a large scale, and certainly not within the short time window when terminal lucidity tends to spontaneously occur. It is therefore indeed extraordinary—and remains unexplained—how it is possible that these patients manifest a return of the very self-awareness and memories that were presumed erased, and cognitive faculties that were presumed lost, shortly before death. As Oscar Bloch, a professor of surgery at the University of Copenhagen Medical School, wrote in a review of earlier cases in 1903:

It was nothing new that the mentally ill could have episodes when they are perfectly healthy. . . . If such a mentally ill person dies in a lucid period, he dies just like a healthy person. If, however, one who has been mentally ill for years, who just sat there apathetically, as if the world didn't exist for him, who lived more like an animal than like a human, who didn't even possess an animal's level of intelligence, if such a person suddenly shows signs of reason—and this happens shortly before his death—one should rightfully be surprised.[2]

Lessons of Surprise: A Research Workshop at the National Institute on Aging

Now, for the scientist, to be "rightfully surprised" translates into something vital: it means that we observe phenomena that contradict our predictions—predictions made on the grounds of our scientific theories. Such phenomena—should the surprise be indeed "rightful," i.e., based on real and reliable observations—would therefore render a given theory most likely deficient and in need of expansion or correction, or outright false. This process of theory testing is called falsification, and it is generally considered the gold standard for testing and judging the truth value of a theory: a theory is only as good and valid as it makes correct predictions (given that these are made on sufficient knowledge of background facts) based on the laws or regularities it describes. And indeed: How are such cases in which a severely diseased brain coexists with a clear, lucid mind possible? After all, such cases confront us with observations that suggest the antithesis, as it were, to Paul Edwards's notion of the terminal decline and destruction of Mrs. D's self as a result of her neurological disorder.

Perhaps, then, the swan song for the weaver was premature. Perhaps loom and weaver may not be identical after all, just as Eccles proposed. And think of the implications. If Provine's nihilist manifesto was largely based on "first taking away the soul," what would it mean to rediscover and reacknowledge it ("second, the soul returns")?

Clearly, something extraordinary is happening here. And yet, it took more than one hundred years after Bloch's musings until terminal lucidity caught the attention of researchers—and at long last, the National Institute on Aging at the National Institute of Health in Bethesda, Maryland, held an international expert research workshop on terminal lucidity in the summer of 2018 (the National Institute on Aging Workshop on Paradoxical Lucidity in Late-Stage Dementia). We were a small group of nine researchers from a number of disciplines—neurologists, psycholinguists, nursing researchers, psychiatrists, and psychologists—who gathered for this expert workshop to discuss terminal (or, as the workshop organizers preferred to call it: paradoxical) lucidity and develop research strategies for its exploration. Under the courteous and encouraging guidance of our hosts, supervisory medical officer Basil Eldadah, Division of Geriatrics and Clinical Gerontology at the NIA, health scientist administrator Elena Fazio, Division of Behavioral and Social Research, and program officer Kristina McLinden, Division of Neuroscience, we discussed what we thus far knew about the enigmatic phenomenon. It wasn't much—I presented some of our preliminary results from my own early research work into terminal lucidity, and others weighed in with their personal observations or research ideas based on their own clinical or research work.

We spent wonderful days in Bethesda; days in which my colleagues and I finally met like-minded people who were engaged in research on a topic about which virtually nothing was yet known—and which was met with outright skepticism by some of our colleagues. There was a pioneering spirit in the air that one rarely has the fortune to experience. While the researcher's everyday work consists of searching for new connections and refining existing theories and models, he or she rarely has the intellectually satisfying pleasure of stumbling upon a phenomenon that has revolutionary implications on several levels at once. I think each of us realized in some way that we, as a small group, were working on a research topic that could potentially change the life, and alleviate the suffering, of millions. Our work could touch upon so many aspects and layers of being human—and of *remaining* human even in the face of a debilitating neurological disorder.

Discussions continued during lunch breaks and subsequent dinners and walks after the actual seminar days: What was this all about? What does it mean? Are there ways to utilize a yet undiscovered cause of terminal lucidity for the treatment of the dementias and other severe neurological disorders? And before it comes to that—what *is* terminal, or paradoxical, lucidity?

To come even close to attempting to answer the many questions raised by terminal lucidity, it was the latter question that was to be answered first: our main task consisted in finding an initial formal definition of paradoxical, or terminal, lucidity, on the basis of which further systematic research could be conducted:

> An episode of unexpected, spontaneous, meaningful, and relevant communication or connectedness in a patient who is assumed to have permanently lost the capacity for coherent verbal or behavioral interaction due to a progressive and pathophysiologic dementing process.[3]

In other words, there are seemingly hopeless cases of mental and cognitive impairment due to brain disorders that unexpectedly disabuse us of previously held notions—both in terms of clinical prognosis and with regard to the fate of the person, or the self, in dementia and similar disorders. For these cases seem to tell us: not only can the inner self of even a severely cognitively impaired person occasionally become visible to and through the "eyes of love." It also can reveal itself—and with unmistakable clarity—toward the end of life of these patients. And then, it shines through. It returns, in some cases after years of being lost and, so it seemed to bystanders, destroyed. And not only does it return, it frequently appears to be fully aware of the fact that its return takes place in the very last days or hours of life. This, then, is what terminal lucidity is about: returning to say farewell.

In the following, I will present a few exemplary case reports from a great variety of different and independent sources for the reader to form a better idea of what this phenomenon typically entails and what it actually looks like. The following examples come from a time span of more than 120 years, were noted in different countries and by different professionals (oncologists, psychiatrists, neurologists, biologists, ministers), and occurred in the context of very different underlying brain disorders—and yet they are all remarkably similar in telling a different story about personhood, brain damage, and death than materialism tells.

The Laurenz Case

The following early case report by the Berlin physician Rudolf Leubuscher is taken from German biologist Michael Nahm's historical case collection.[4] In his 1846 article "Return of the Consciousness of a Madwoman before Death,"[5] Leubuscher describes the case of a forty-four-year-old patient (Ms. Laurenz), who was admitted to his institution. Ms. Laurenz suffered from prolonged states of disorientation and severe delusions. During her inpatient treatment, her condition worsened progressively—she suffered from intense dizziness and amnesia, and was very confused. She claimed to be twenty-two years old, never to have had a family (the forty-four-year-old was in fact the widowed mother of five), and was convinced that her mother had been dead for fifty years.

A few months after her admission, her doctors noted a slight improvement in her dizziness and fainting spells. However, Ms. Laurenz remained severely confused and clung to her delusional ideas. In due course, her mental state continued to deteriorate and her dizziness and fainting spells increased once again. After another bout in late September 1845, she was profoundly confused for a period of some four months. She eventually died in February 1846. However, Leubuscher notes in his case report that, as death approached, Laurenz suddenly woke up to a "free and clear consciousness":

> She is once again aware of her entire past, no longer confuses her surroundings as before, shows deep and heartfelt recognition for the attention she receives, apologizes for being a burden as a result of her uncleanliness, and dies in the full knowledge that such a miserable existence could be of no more use to the world.[6]

The posthumous autopsy of Laurenz's brain revealed that she had suffered from profound, severe brain damage: a sharp bone fragment of one to two centimeters in length had caused chronic meningitis on the inside of the cranium, as well as a softening of cystic appearance to the cerebral membrane. Furthermore, blistery deposits in several brain areas, as well as edema in the cerebral ventricles were found. Leubuscher's notes on this diagnosis therefore say:

> We find a brain disease that, according to other pathological experience, eliminates higher cognitive functioning, and which in fact had that effect for years, with little variation in mental activity [. . .] and we find the return of mental activity to its earlier integrity under unchanged organic conditions, which, at least according to the anatomical diagnosis, did not allow for the assumption of significant regeneration.[7]

The Case of Anna Katharina Ehmer, Known as Käthe[8]

One of the more prominent cases of terminal lucidity (also from Michael Nahm's case collection, and frequently discussed in literature) is that of Anna Katharina Ehmer, usually simply known as Käthe. Käthe, born on May 30, 1895, began suffering from prolonged seizures at the age of six weeks and only learned to walk at the age of two and a half years. At the age of six, on June 17, 1901, she was admitted to the psychiatric ward at Hephata in Treysa, Hesse (Germany), where she spent the remainder of her life until her death on March 1, 1922. The following is from her case file:

> Käthe was a born idiot and never learned to speak a word. She stared at some random spot for hours, or fidgeted for hours on end. She gobbled food, excreted, emitted an animal cry, and slept. We have not observed any other stirrings of life on her part in all those long years. Never did we notice her participate in the life around her for as much as a second. She also deteriorated physically: one leg had to be amputated and her infirmity only increased.[9]

In the morning of March 1, 1922—the day of Käthe's death—the nurse told her treating physician that "it looked like she might soon die, for the girl had been humming to herself for quite a while."[10] The resident physician, Wilhelm Wittneben, gave the following account of Käthe's death:

> As we entered the death chamber, we couldn't believe our eyes and ears: the born idiot Käthe sang her own death songs. "Where finds the soul her home, her peace? Peace,

peace, celestial peace!" Käthe sang for half an hour. Her face
was spiritual, transfigured. Then she quietly went to sleep.
The doctor who, like the nurse, had tears in his eyes, kept
saying: "I am before a medical mystery. If required to do so, I
can prove, by means of a section, that Käthe's cerebral cortex
was utterly destroyed and that cogitation was anatomically
impossible."

Käthe, therefore, only appeared not to notice any of the
goings-on around her. In fact, she had visibly taken in quite
a bit of what took place. For where would she have taken
the text and tune of the song, if not her surroundings? And
she had understood the purport of the song and used it in
the decisive hour of her life. It did seem like a miracle. What
appeared to be even more of a miracle was that the hitherto
utterly dumb Käthe could suddenly render the song's words
clearly and distinctly, even though, caused by numerous on-
sets of meningitis, such pervasive anatomical changes to the
cerebral cortex had occurred that it is not rationally comprehensible how the dying girl could suddenly sing clearly,
distinctly, and with comprehension.[11]

Nahm and Greyson have, in the course of their extensive literature
research, found more than eighty such case histories in the older medical literature of the last 250 years.[12] The majority of these cases were
described before the end of the nineteenth century—only a few works
on the subject of terminal lucidity appeared thereafter.

But as Sandy Mcleod points out in a brief historical overview, TL
also found its way into the chronicles of art and cultural history, such
as the case of Queen Dagmar of Denmark (thirteenth century) who
was in a coma yet briefly awoke at her deathbed as her husband King
Valdemar returned from a hunting trip. The story became legend and
was later painted by Georg von Rosen in 1898.[13] And when Russian

writer Pushkin died of sepsis of his injuries incurred in a pistol duel, he encountered, according to the attending physician, "one of those sudden turns for the better that is so illusory of fatal illness" shortly before his death.[14]

Contemporary Cases

The overlap between historical and artistic and medical case descriptions is perhaps no coincidence—about a hundred years ago, physicians often wrote wonderfully detailed, sometimes almost literary works about individual patients or diseases. Today, however, medical protocols look much more sober, as professional standards precisely specify what belongs in such a protocol and what does not. And for a good reason. The aim is primarily to use a uniform language and to thus make it easier for colleagues who read the patient reports to grasp all the essential information at a glance. On the one hand, such writing enables a well-coordinated and efficient way of offering medical help to patients; on the other, it comes with some costs as a purely diagnostic or therapeutic view clearly does not take into account the larger picture of the personhood and individuality of a patient beyond his illness (and recovery, survival, or death). The fact that medical writing changed quite a bit during the past century should not suggest that terminal lucidity is a thing of the past that can be written off as an artifact due to, for example, misdiagnoses, romanticizing or sanctimonious narratives, and the like. The fact that the phenomenon—until recently—is less often referred to in medical literature does not mean that it no longer occurs. It does, and recent research has filled in the gap of decades of neglect.

Since my research interest in this topic has become publicly known, I have repeatedly heard from doctors or nurses who told me that they had witnessed terminal lucidity—only they did not include it in the patient protocols, because they did not know how to formulate this in the medical language of usual protocols: "And then something very unusual happened, for which unfortunately we have no technical term and which is currently not described in any textbook: the patient regained her memory and there was a heartrendingly beautiful last encounter with her family members shortly before she passed away. Nobody understood what happened; but it was beautiful." For better or worse, this is not what patient protocols usually look like today. Perhaps our and others' work on terminal lucidity will help to foster a new culture of how we observe and appreciate the individual differences in how patients experience their illness, their lives, and also their deaths. It is, after all, quite telling that for the past hundred years or so, an unknown number of patients displayed very unusual behavior at their deathbed, and yet others come forth with their own experiences only after research articles officially "confirm" that terminal lucidity really does happen (and has a name).

But as we shall see, the phenomenon itself is not limited to specific historical epochs; and neither is it limited to particular geographical areas or medical cultures: to this date, my research group has collected contemporary reports from many European countries, the United States, Russia, India, South Korea, Japan, New Zealand, Nigeria, and China.

Addressing these more recent cases, an example from my own case collection, which took place in early 2019, is summarized below as reported by the daughter of an elderly German lady stricken by Alzheimer's:

> My mother had advanced Alzheimer's. She no longer recognized us, and she didn't even seem to care who these "strangers" were visiting her once or twice a week. On the day before her passing, however, everything was different. Not only did she recognize us—she wanted to know what

had happened in the course of the past year for every one of us, delighting in good news and shed the odd tear over bad news (just as this affectionate, motherly woman had done before her dementia). Her comments were as wise and caring as ever. When she heard that my younger daughter had recently broken off her engagement and descended into a deep depression, she asked her to stay with her for a while afterward, because she wanted to talk to her in private. My daughter never told me what she discussed with my mother, but it was a turning point for her. When we took our leave, we didn't know what to expect next: Was she miraculously healed of her dementia? With hindsight, however, I believe that my siblings and me understood that she knew exactly that she didn't have long to live. She said goodbye to every one of us, held our hands, stroking them with her thumb (just as she had done when we were children). She was—I can't think of another way to say this—simply her old self. Sadly, it wasn't meant to last. She died the same night.

Nahm et al. (2012) report another contemporary case of a middle-aged patient with a brain tumor:

In a case recently reported to us, a forty-two-year-old investment manager had a grand mal seizure "out of the blue" one night. Although his EEG showed generalized slowing, repeated MRIs appeared normal. Two months later, however, a repeat MRI showed a plum-sized glioblastoma multiforme. By the time he had surgery two weeks later, the tumor had doubled in size and a second had formed in his speech center. Following two surgical excisions, gamma knife radiation, intrathecal chemotherapy, and steroids, he was able to go back to work part-time. However, the tumor soon recurred, and after a failed trial of an experimental oral chemotherapy agent, he declined further treatment and enrolled in hospice care in his home. He quickly became bedridden, blind in one eye, incontinent, and increasingly incoherent in his speech and bizarre in his behavior. He appeared to be unable to make sense of his surroundings, and when his family touched him, he would slap as if at an insect. He eventually stopped sleeping, talking deliriously through the night.

After several weeks of that, he suddenly one night appeared calm and started speaking coherently, and then slept peacefully. The following morning he remained coherent and conversed with his wife, discussing his imminent death with her for the first time. However, he stopped speaking later that day, and lay immobile in his bed, not eating or drinking for two more weeks, after which he expired after several hours of status epilepticus.[15]

How often do such lucid returns actually happen? We do not know, as the phenomenon, let alone its prevalence, hasn't been exhaustively researched yet. But in a study recently carried out by the British psychiatrist Peter Fenwick, no fewer than seven out of ten caregivers stated that they have, in the course of their work in a hospice, observed cases of unexpected mental clarity in their dying patients.[16] The gold standard, however, to establish how often a medical event occurs is to conduct a so-called prospective study—that is, you do not study events after they occurred (called retrospective study), but carefully observe and follow a predefined group of patients who could, in principle, be candidates for the phenomenon you are looking for, not knowing whether any—or how many—of these patients would display it.

In 2009, Sandy Macleod did just that: he monitored one hundred successive deaths in a hospice in New Zealand, and found six cases of terminal lucidity preceding the patients' deaths by up to forty-eight hours. Of these cases, three had brain involvement, four were acutely delirious, and one patient had required high-dosage opioid therapy—in other words, a sizable number of these patients were cognitively impaired due to illness or other physiological factors. And yet, they, too, experienced terminal lucidity, as the following case report by Macleod illustrates:

> A seventy-two-year-old retired electrician presented the previous year with persistent cough. Chest X-ray indicated a lung lesion which was determined to be non–small cell carcinoma. Six months after a lobectomy he suffered an epileptic seizure. Whole brain irradiation palliated the symptoms of cerebral metastases for a further six months at which time he developed an uncontrollable series of major seizures and left upper limb weakness. Corticosteroids and anticonvulsants promptly relieved the cerebral symptoms and signs though within weeks his neurology had progressed. On admission to the hospice he was aphasic, doubly incontinent, had a dense hemiplegia, and had fitted the previous night. He could no longer comply with his oral medications. A parenteral [subcutaneous] regime of midazolam (45mg SC/24hours) to replace oral phenytoin, morphine (20mg SC/24hours) for chest pain, dexamethasone (4mg SC/24hours), and haloperidol (3mg/24 hours) for nausea, was introduced. His clinical state settled for thirty-six hours, though the neurological signs only partially remitted. Then remarkably he regained speech and became alert and verbally responsive to his family. Within twelve hours he lapsed into a coma and died the following day peacefully.[17]

As already mentioned, such case reports were until recently for the most part confined to historical medical literature and are occasionally scattered in more recent medical writing; they have only become the subject of systematic scientific research in very recent years. At the time of writing—January 2023—no more than a dozen original articles on the subject have been published in scientific and medical journals. In the following discussion, I will draw both on survey data and personal letters and mail I was sent by people who have witnessed episodes of terminal lucidity.

A Gift Wrapped in Pain

Ever since several newspapers and magazines and, subsequently, radio and TV stations began reporting on my research, I regularly have been contacted by people who wrote or told me about the unexpected return of the very person whose deterioration and final decline they had witnessed.

Theirs is yet another perspective on the phenomenon, next to the perspective of perplexed doctors and nurses or curious researchers. More than a few of the relatives and friends of those who witnessed terminal lucidity tell us that they feel lonely and isolated with the memory of this experience, or worse, that they feel misunderstood by most people when they try to relate to others what they have witnessed. After all, until a few years ago, there wasn't even a term—terminal lucidity—to describe these occurrences; even though, as we have seen, historical overviews suggest that episodes of terminal lucidity have been reported during the past centuries. Yet the lack of a name for these lucid moments before death, as well as the fact that they remain unexplained, all too often means that those who are moved to talk about their experience are met with incomprehension or ignorance, or remain silent altogether.

Terminal lucidity can be an ambivalent experience for witnesses. On the one hand, those who report witnessing TL treasure what they have seen. It will remain with them as a cherished memory. They have experienced something unquestionably extraordinary, albeit, as our research suggests (more on that in the following chapter), probably not infrequent. On the other hand, they were, until the first reports on the systematic research into this phenomenon were published in the scientific literature a few years ago, literally at a loss for words when it came to specifying, describing, classifying—and sometimes even believing—what they had witnessed; and, alongside the lack of words, they often lacked the very means to share their experience with others. How do you think about, talk about, and even begin to understand an extraordinary event that, until recently, lacked a name? And yet, many of these witnesses tell us that what they saw has had a profound impact on their life and specifically on their view of personal identity, memory, and the self. Many of them opt for a less restrained wording than that. Rather, they tell us that they had an encounter with the preserved self or soul of their loved one—the very soul or inner self that for so long had been "hidden" or rendered inaccessible by dementia or a similarly devastating brain disorder. And a few go even further than that—they talk about the spiritual and religious implications of what they witnessed.

I will return to this in later chapters of this book. For the moment, however, we clearly are confronted with a phenomenon that comes with a number of potentially significant implications and questions on personhood, the soul, and death and dying.

4

Setting the Scene

Studying, but Above All: Listening

Terminal lucidity raises enough questions to merit further and more thorough research. The eyewitness reports on TL ought to be taken seriously in the first place even if—or because—we currently understand so very little about TL. We need to listen to those who witnessed it; not despite the fact that they experienced something unusual, but precisely because of it. At the same time, from a research perspective, we also need to apply some caution when it comes to drawing conclusions on these reports. For extraordinary claims, as a general rule, require, if not extraordinary, then at least good evidence, which means: reasonably reliable and, ideally, verifiable data. And the claim that a number of patients who suffer from severe cognitive impairment due to "irreversible" brain damage would have sudden and renewed access to their memories, that they would be able to think, speak, and act again as if they are experiencing a full spontaneous healing of what are held to be incurable disorders just hours or days before their eventual death—such a claim is extraordinary in more than one way.

But is there also extraordinary, or at least sufficiently good evidence supporting this claim? Granted, there exists a sizable number of individual case reports and stories. These are moving stories, and such stories deserve to be heard, acknowledged, taken seriously. That is the human and humane side of it. However, from a research perspective, things get more complicated. In scientific research, individual reports ("anecdotes")—no matter how informative or groundbreaking they may be—are generally considered to be rather weak evidence (and—evidence for what?). Anyone who has studied the weakness and unreliability of eyewitness reports knows that our memories are error-prone and that people sometimes are utterly convinced of having witnessed something that they in fact never saw or experienced.

Additionally, even in today's high-tech medicine, mistakes happen: patients are misdiagnosed or receive the wrong medication, which will exacerbate rather than alleviate symptoms. People err. And when people err, they may come up with moving, beautiful stories—moving and beautiful, but not exactly accurate. These are some of the reasons why what is called "anecdotal" evidence is usually considered to be weak evidence, if it is considered to be evidence at all—especially if it would argue against some widely held notions such as the irreversibility of the various dementias.

At the same time, we cannot afford to dismiss individual case reports altogether. After all, it was precisely such anecdotal accounts which, for example, have led to the discovery of new diseases (remember that both HIV and Covid-19 started from very small clusters, reported as individual observations and case histories or anecdotes). And some groundbreaking medical discoveries began as anecdotal reports, such as the discovery of the smallpox vaccine: British physician Edward Jenner had informally observed that individuals infected with the harmless cowpox virus were protected from the immeasurably more dangerous smallpox virus, presumably as a result of a cross-reaction of antibodies to the cowpox virus.[1]

But anecdotal "evidence" often did, and does, lead to some dire scientific fallacies (think of most "alternative" medicine which, while reporting "successful" cure anecdotes aplenty, almost invariably fails when testing efficacy under rigorous conditions).

In other words: much can succeed, but just as much can go wrong if one relies on small numbers and individual observations. Recollections can be unreliable; wishful thinking can compromise impartial reports and sober analysis, compounded by the lack of controlled conditions that may enable us to recognize phenomena as what they are (as opposed to what they seem to be).

It is therefore unsurprising that the scientific and medical community's initial reaction to the first contemporary overviews of historical TL cases was one of restrained curiosity, interest, caution, and sometimes downright skepticism in equal measure. Given what we currently know about the dementias in particular, and the relationship between mental, cognitive, and neuronal functions in general, the phenomenon is extremely unlikely. The dementias are considered decidedly irreversible conditions caused by permanent and irreparable erosion of brain tissue, which in turn causes irreversible disintegration of the mind and cognition. There has been no evidence of reversal of the neuronal causes of dementia. Yet with terminal lucidity, the observed spontaneous remission would suggest just that. Such a reversal would require that large cell formations somehow spontaneously regrow—and not only "somehow" regrow, but do so in an organized manner, into the functional networks of the patient's brain, so that he or she regains access to full memory and cognitive function. And given that the patient will die within a few hours or days, such a regeneration mechanism would make little functional and evolutionary sense.

Hence the skepticism about terminal lucidity: an extraordinary claim, without extraordinary evidence. Until the first general overviews of historical case histories were published in a number of medical journals, such skepticism was understandable.

A further reason for scientific skepticism is that TL plays into religious and spiritual intuitions and hopes. Just as Paul Edwards's case example of Mrs. D's fate was intended to be a powerful—and seemingly compelling—argument for materialist reductionism, terminal lucidity lends itself to a dualist interpretation of "liberation of the soul" from the shackles of an impaired body, especially the brain.

This state of affairs continued for a while. The first historical and some more recent overview works had been published, but serious research was prompted by the growing chorus of people who worked in the helping professions, i.e., in hospices, palliative care units, or nursing homes for dementia. The readers' comments section under the few articles on TL that appeared on science and medical web blogs and online news testified this putatively "historical" phenomenon wasn't a result of outdated medical practice:

> Why does the article state that such things were only observed in past centuries? My father's brother had, before our very eyes, experienced a fulminant reawakening from his advanced dementia hours before his death. We were all speechless. He looked at us with a clear gaze, called us by our names, and bade us farewell and died the same night.

> Us nurses, we know this. We always say "the last glow has begun." Only the week before last, we had a case like this on the ward. Historical—my foot.

Similar messages appeared in the online portals of various self-help groups for family members of patients with dementia or other severe neurological disorders. Even so—touching and credible as some of these testimonials were—their evidential value didn't rank significantly above the historical reports that had been quoted in the first historical reviews on older TL cases. And yet, little strokes fell big oaks—and with the growing number of contemporary reports of TL, the phenomenon slowly began to receive more attention from the scientific community.

Encounters

For example, in November 2014, the American psychologist Jesse Bering dedicated his popular and widely read column "Bering in Mind," published in *Scientific American,* to the phenomenon. Bering used his short piece to describe what was at this point known about TL, addressing his discussion to the whole spectrum of its implications, including the relationship between mind and brain. Bering may have been particularly receptive to TL, having witnessed a few years prior a similar episode in his own family:

> I'm as sworn to radical rationalism as the next neo-Darwinian materialist. That said, over the years I've had to "quarantine," for lack of a better word, a few anomalous personal experiences that have stubbornly defied my own logical understanding of them. [. . .] When my mother died in early 2000, we had a final farewell that some researchers might consider paranormal. At the time, it did strike me as remarkable—and after all these years, I still can't talk about it without getting emotional. The night before she died at the age of fifty-four (after a long battle with ovarian cancer), I was sleeping in my mother's bedroom alongside her. The

truth was that I'd already grieved her loss a few days earlier, from the moment she lapsed into what the hospice nurses had assured us was an irretrievable coma. So at this point, waiting for her body to expire as a physical machine wasn't as difficult as the loss of "her" beforehand, which is when I'd completely broken down. It had all happened so quickly and, I suppose being young and in denial about how imminent her death really was, I hadn't actually gotten around to telling her how very grateful I was to have had her as my mom and how much I loved her. But then, around 3 A.M., I awoke to find her reaching her hand out to me, and she seemed very much aware. She was too weak to talk but her eyes communicated all. We spent about five minutes holding hands: me sobbing, kissing her cheeks, telling her everything I'd meant to say before but hadn't. Soon she closed her eyes again, this time for good. She died the next day. I didn't quite see the experience as "supernatural" when it happened. And I'm not sure I do today either. But I also didn't have a name for the experience then. In fact, one didn't even exist. It does now: terminal lucidity. [. . .] I remain a skeptic. Still, I really don't know how my mother managed those five minutes of perfect communion with me when, ostensibly, all of her cognitive functions were already lost. Was it her immortal soul? One last firestorm in her dying brain? Honestly, I'm just glad it happened.[2]

I owe my own interest in TL to a similar experience. I was still a student at the University of Vienna when the following happened, several years before the first articles on the subject of TL were published: My grandmother suffered from what was most likely cardiovascular dementia. In her last year, she was hardly able to speak and no longer capable of initiating a conversation, or adequately answering even simple questions. Yet one day, my mother phoned and asked me to immediately call my grandmother in Geneva, Switzerland: "We just had a wonderful conversation. I do not know what happened—but you should call."

I call my grandmother, and she answers the phone—she sounds tired and gentle, but she is perfectly clear and as gracious, caring, and affectionate as she used to be before her health declined. She greets me. We talk. And I thank her for the wonderful days we children spent with our grandparents in Geneva, where my mother's parents moved from Germany in order to escape the war and the collective madness that befell Germany during the Nazi reign. She, in turn, thanks me (and my brother) for the many beautiful experiences we shared together: "You brought so much joy to our lives," she almost whispers. But no—*you* brought so much joy and warmth to ours. Thank you. And we talk about the wonderful memories we share. I had so many reasons to thank her.

Then she moves to the present day. She knows why she is taken care of by the nurses. And she adds that she's been very tired over the past months—and that she hardly remembers them at all. Our conversation lasts some ten minutes; she is perfectly lucid throughout, doesn't show a trace of confusion or forgetfulness. In short, during our conversation, she is once more the gentle and affectionate and warm grandmother I remembered from my childhood and adolescent days—and was now allowed to experience once more. Once more meeting her old self; herself. On the one hand, that whole episode was wonderful; on the other, it was heartrending, because I (in fact, I now believe both of us) sensed at the time that this gift of spending time together, if only on the phone, would be transient, and the conversation our last. It was.

Hearing the Call

As it happens, only a few weeks before this incident, I sat in on one of the last university lectures given by the Austrian psychiatrist and neurologist Viktor Frankl at Vienna Medical School. Then over ninety, Frankl was best known for his Holocaust testimony *Man's Search for Meaning,* and had authored several groundbreaking works on psychiatric and psychological anthropology in which he develops and argues for a scientifically informed, yet non-reductionist account of human personhood.[3] It is in this context that Viktor Frankl articulated the so-called "psychiatric credo": the unconditional faith in the trans-morbid, or incorruptible nature and dignity of the noetic or "inner" person of each human being as a directive and guideline for humane medical practice. Frankl thus differentiates between the psychophysiological organism on the one hand, and the conscious individual self on the other hand, the inner core of each human being:

> The spiritual or noetic person can be affected and impaired—but not destroyed—by a psychophysical disorder. What a disorder can destroy, what it can subvert, is the psychophysical organism alone. [. . .] The subversion of the organism, therefore, represents no less—but also no more—than an obstruction of the access to the person—no more than that. And this shall be our psychiatric credo: this unconditional faith in the person, this "blind" faith in the "invisible," but indestructible noetic person. And if I didn't have this faith, I would prefer not to be a doctor.[4]

When my grandmother and I had our last conversation, I did not know at that time what and how it happened. I only was grateful for the unexpected gift of a last and wonderful conversation. But perhaps I was not as unprepared as many other witnesses I later interviewed and corresponded with; I had heard of Frankl's notion of an incorruptible inner person beyond and behind disease and disorder, and the previously quoted phone conversation with John C. Eccles, had taken place only a few months before.

However, Frankl (like Eccles) expressly spoke of a credo, an assumption that doesn't lend itself to further empirical investigation or verification. And I was also aware that the Holocaust survivor Frankl, less than four years after the end of the Holocaust and his own liberation from his last concentration camp (part of the Dachau complex), deliberately proposed this firm belief in the incorruptible personal dignity of the human person as a counterpoint to the havoc of the so-called "euthanasia" perpetrated by Hitler and the National Socialists. Frankl's credo that the most cognitively impaired, even comatose person remains human did and does indeed represent a stark counterpoint to fascism. According to this view, what constitutes personhood is not a person's functional capacity. Personhood, after all, is not ours to determine or to ascribe or deny to someone, but something we can merely come upon, acknowledge, respect, and honor. Each person, especially a frail person who may temporarily or permanently be unable to look after himself, calls us to devote ourselves to him and never to lose faith in the existence and dignity of the inner person behind the facade of illness and frailty.

When I tried to make sense of my last conversation with my grandmother, I also recalled a lecture by the Swiss-American psychiatrist and pioneer of thanatology, Elisabeth Kübler-Ross. She and her medical team had observed how confused patients (primarily cancer patients) had, in numerous cases, demonstrated increased vitality and clarity of mind shortly before their death.[5] This phenomenon is interesting in its own right, though perhaps not as mystifying as the spontaneous remission and resurgence of a lucid mind in cases of severe neurological and cognitive impairment. As it happens, Kübler-Ross also indicated that she occasionally observed patients with severe dementia regain clarity before death—but left it at this allusion—without, as far as I am aware, ever probing further into what were, in all likelihood, occasional cases of terminal lucidity in her own case collection.

As for me, there was a time in my own early academic career when I was confronted with the possibility that something remarkable could be happening at the hour of death of patients who were neurologically ill and cognitively impaired. I had learned of Frankl's psychiatric credo, heard Eccles's forceful plea to acknowledge the transcendent nature of the conscious self, and recalled Kübler-Ross's observations only weeks or months before I had my final conversation with my grandmother. And this conversation certainly lent a face to these allusions, for I now had firsthand experience with an event that apparently supported these notions. I had witnessed that my grandmother's self and personality had outlived her severely compromised neurological function, and somehow "reappeared" shortly before she died. Something, at any rate, had happened to enable the old self to resurface against all medical odds. And this, in turn, seemed to corroborate Frankl's and Eccles's claim that the self does not entirely fall victim to physical illness, decline, and decay.

And yet, although I had witnessed something extraordinary and had encountered theoretical notions that would have helped me make sense of what I experienced, I did not pursue the matter any further. The last conversation with my grandmother remained an inexplicable personal experience I occasionally looked back on—grateful often, mystified sometimes, but no more than that.

Fast forward perhaps ten years or so: As mentioned earlier, in 2009, the first peer-reviewed articles on TL were published in the *Journal of Nervous and Mental Disease,* the journal *Palliative & Supportive Care,* and the *Journal of Near-Death Studies* and it dawned on me that my erstwhile experience had in fact been part of a much greater phenomenon. Hence, when I read these first reports about terminal lucidity, apart from the obvious scientific curiosity—I was now teaching theory of cognitive science at University of Vienna—it was the memories of my own encounter that made me pause and wonder. The time had come to confront what I had seen and heard, to better understand what I experienced ten years earlier. And apart from these personal motives, the possible implications of terminal lucidity seemed so very significant—from both a clinical and a philosophical point of view; far too significant, in fact, to simply keep ignoring the subject. I wanted to learn more about it—but, alas, there was not much material available to draw on. Very few studies on the subject had been published. Moreover, as already mentioned, the majority of these studies dealt with cases that had occurred one or two centuries ago. There were hardly any contemporary case reports, though according to the prospective study by Macleod (2009)[6]—until then the only prospective study of this phenomenon—one could assume that some 6 percent of dying patients (albeit including those without impairments to their central nervous system) would experience an episode of terminal lucidity of varying duration shortly before their death. The phenomenon apparently occurred in a small segment of patients, but it was not extremely rare. Still, it was not possible to estimate, based on Macleod's data, how often such cases would arise in a predefined patient population of dementia sufferers or otherwise "incurable" neurologically afflicted persons.

The publication of the three first articles on TL serendipitously coincided with the end of the summer semester 2009 in Vienna. I always use the end of the term—once the main material from lectures and seminars has been worked through and students are overburdened with preparing for exams and term papers—to discuss lesser-known findings, new research methods, and in fact anything that may not—or not yet—be mandatory study material. And so I used one of the last afternoon sessions of my cognitive science seminar at University of Vienna to introduce TL and to relay what I then knew about it.

It wasn't much; but it was enough to understand that something very unusual happens in such cases. It didn't escape my students that TL was indeed a remarkable phenomenon with a potentially enormous range of both theoretical and clinical implications. And just as I had hoped, my presentation provoked a lively debate, which we continued after the end of the seminar at a nearby café.

By late afternoon of the same day, a group of students volunteered to assist me in further researching contemporary cases of terminal lucidity. That was the beginning of a scientific, and soon philosophical, endeavor and adventure. At the time, I had no idea where it would take me.

PART II

Terminal Lucidity

It is the hour of witness that is coming,
very calm and very complete:
a hope which seems close to being realized.
—Henri de Lubac

5

Approaching Terminal Lucidity: The Pilot Study and Its Aftermath

Searching for a Phenomenon

When one is trying to understand a phenomenon that is poorly understood and about which very little is known, the first task is to systematically capture as much as possible of and about the phenomenon itself. The available material did not yet lend itself to that. The historical case reports collected by Nahm and Greyson, as well as some other reports that I had found in older works at the Vienna Medical School's library, were heterogeneous in their presentation: different in length, different in quality, and especially different in what exactly was described, and how.

A reliable description, let alone a definition on the basis of the available reports was thus practically impossible. The fact that a number of patients, some of whom suffered from severe cognitive impairment for years on end, may experience a sudden return of their cognitive functions was the only common denominator. Beyond that, no two reports were alike—not, it seemed, because the individual cases were so very different, but because the authors had paid attention to different aspects of the lucid episodes of their patients.

This shortcoming thus provided a clear path forward: namely, to develop a simple methodology that—instead of merely collecting recent cases and extending the range of highly heterogeneous reports—would allow us to systematically describe and compare them, so that further research could focus on what actually happened before, during, and after a TL episode. In other words, we needed to develop a questionnaire that required entry of specific characteristics and parameters in order to collect a sufficient number of comparable contemporary case reports. I therefore began to design a questionnaire that included an inventory of those items that were missing in some of the historical reports, such as demographical data of the patients, their medical diagnosis, their cognitive and mental state on a typical day before the lucid episode and during the lucid episode, and the duration of the lucid episode, as well as the time between the lucid episode and the patient's death. Furthermore, in order to avoid memory distortions, we would only collect and analyze cases that were witnessed less than twelve months prior to the completion of the questionnaire.

As a pilot survey—to test the reliability of the (web-based) questionnaire, and to see whether we would find any new cases at all—we initially sent it to hospices, palliative care units, and nursing homes in German-speaking countries (Germany, Austria, Switzerland, and the principality of Liechtenstein). And waited. Anxiously waited, without any idea what to expect; in fact, with no idea whether to expect anything. For at that point it certainly wasn't a given that we would receive any responses or case reports of TL, and if so, how many—and whether there would be enough to obtain at least a first approximation of a phenomenology of terminal lucidity.

But once the questionnaires were sent out, slowly and steadily, the reports trickled in. One by one, the first coming back only a day after we sent the questionnaires. Within a few weeks, I'd received twenty-nine questionnaires, and more followed. Bearing in mind that Nahm and colleagues had found approximately eighty cases spread over a large time window of 250 years in literature, this seemed to suggest that there were more cases than expected. Since I had assumed that we were dealing with a rare occurrence, the number of reports I received in such a small time window was both unanticipated and encouraging.

In addition, analysis of these first cases in our collection mirrored some of the earlier findings reported by Nahm and Greyson: we also found that the TL was not limited to specific types of neurological disorders or diagnoses. While more than half of the case reports we received concerned dementia patients, we also received case reports of patients with brain tumors, traumatic brain injuries, cognitive impairment after strokes, and—rather less specific—severe cognitive impairment without further designator.

At this point, I was keen to know whether other researchers—alerted to the phenomenon by the three articles published in 2009 and some of the follow-up work published since—had turned up similar results. I asked around among my colleagues and other researchers specialized in the psychology of death and dying. But, surprisingly—given that the phenomenon had by now begun to attract at least some attention in the scientific community—it seemed that no other attempts at systematically collecting and analyzing more such cases were taking place. Many had heard of it, some had witnessed it and sent me their own case reports; but no attempts were made to actively pursue more such cases. Or if these attempts were in progress, they flew under the radar of both the public and the grapevine of our research community.

IANDS

At one of the regular table meetings of our informal cognitive science working group, which at that time met in Vienna's Café Florianihof, a colleague eventually advised me to present the results of my pilot study at the annual congress of the International Association for Near-Death Studies (IANDS). Based in Durham, North Carolina, IANDS is the oldest international organization to support research into the physical, psychological, social, and spiritual aspects of near-death experiences, as well as more general research into the psychology of death and dying. Nowadays, IANDS is less involved with scientific research and serves more as a hub for anything both death-related and unusual (including some nonscientific approaches to the topic, being the home both of sober near-death research and shamanic drumming and anything in between). If anywhere, my colleague suggested, I might find like-minded researchers at this hub of death-related fringe interests—possibly including those who had already collected some cases, but still lacked sufficient material to publish their findings. So in 2014, I submitted a presentation of our pilot study findings to be given at the annual IANDS congress in Newport Beach, California. Due to the critical state of a family member who was suffering from advanced cancer, however, I had to cancel my attendance only a few days before the conference. I owe it to the initiative of the very kind and gentle Robert Mays, one of the organizers of the IANDS conference, that my lecture was given nonetheless—by Mays himself, who bravely agreed to present our findings to the audience, with nothing but my scant notes (I usually deliver my lectures extempore) and a PowerPoint presentation to go by. With hindsight, I am grateful that Robert thrust aside my initial skepticism and convinced me that our findings were important and significant enough to merit presentation at the conference, even if I myself was unable to attend and present them in person.

This unusual arrangement, however, had some unexpected consequences. I didn't know when I entrusted my lecture to Robert Mays that he had, independent of our Vienna work, developed an elaborate dualist theory of the human soul[1], and accordingly would exercise much less philosophical caution in his (excellent) presentation of my findings than I had initially intended. As far as Mays was concerned, our data represented a clear confirmation of his conviction that "something"—the soul—outlasts and survives not only neurological disorders, but also the end of all neurological activity—brain death.

I would not have gone that far had I given that talk; and yet I couldn't have expected Robert to give the exact same lecture as I had intended to give.

The consequence, however, was that some of the attending journalists from various internet media and blogs took up the results of our Viennese pilot study. And given the general tendency of popular media and the blogosphere to embellish their reporting, the coverage was rather more sensational than I would have wished for ("proof of life after death" was the thrust of one story line; "Alzheimer's could become curable" that of another. Needless to say, this is neither what I had intended to claim, nor what Robert actually had said in his/our lecture). Rather, as already pointed out, the original purpose of this lecture was to draw attention to the phenomenon as such, and to signal to other researchers that we were interested in joint research efforts and were hoping to collaborate. I therefore wanted to restrain myself when it came to interpretations—about the nature of personhood, say, or the explanatory gaps of materialism in such cases—particularly as we only had a limited number of cases from a pilot study, which made it much too early to come up with any strong clinical or philosophical claims or speculations.

Given IANDS' focus on the near-death experience[2] (NDE), I was keen to learn what NDE researchers thought about possible parallels between TL and near-death experiences and, more specifically, possible parallels to the occasionally reported positive cognitive changes within near-death experiences. I especially wondered about this point as I had just published a study on near-death experiencers who reported that, during their experience, they felt extremely lucid—sometimes even more than in their usual wakeful state—a finding I will discuss further in the next chapter. It remains to be seen whether this is a merely coincidental parallel between the near-death experience and terminal lucidity, or whether it points to a common phenomenon of the mind at death.

6

"We Need to Talk": The Loneliness of Witnessing the Unexpected

Lifting the Veil

What I couldn't and didn't foresee, however, was the following: Within days after these articles were available online, and the news about my interest in TL spread, I received dozens of letters and emails containing even more reports by those who had witnessed terminal lucidity in their relatives, friends, or patients. I had anticipated and hoped for some additional reports, but was not prepared for so many. To some extent, the situation at that time resembled that of near-death experiencers before Raymond Moody coined the term in his famous book *Life After Life,*[1] published in 1975. We now know that between 8 percent and 18 percent of those who have survived a serious, life-threatening medical crisis and have been resuscitated undergo a near-death experience.[2] In addition, the number of successful resuscitations has significantly increased in tandem with advances in emergency medicine since the early 1970s, which in turn resulted in an increased number of individuals experiencing and reporting their NDE (though, as further studies show, NDEs have been reported for centuries).[3]

When Raymond Moody first attempted to present the phenomenon in a more systematic manner, he had, by his own account, some doubts whether additional cases could be found—precisely because they were so relatively rarely reported. There wasn't even a word for it. But, only two years later, Moody noted that he had collected so many cases since the publication of *Life After Life* that he had difficulties keeping up with analyzing and evaluating them. What had happened? Something quite simple: as already discussed, those who have undergone an extraordinary, profound, and often life-altering experience might doubt themselves, their experience, and ultimately their memory of their experience, as long as they cannot find the words to talk about it. The very fact that the term "near-death experience" created the necessary vocabulary to communicate this profound event opened the floodgates. People who had lived through such an experience could finally talk about it: "This is what I experienced. I am not alone. There is a name for what I have been through."

The media coverage of the IANDS paper prompted a similar reaction. When the first reports were published (and the articles used the term "terminal lucidity"), the floodgates opened. Accounts arrived not only from those who had witnessed terminal lucidity as family members or friends, but also from healthcare professionals and employees of hospices, palliative care units, or nursing homes for cognitively impaired patients. Within days I received (and keep receiving) dozens of letters like the following:

> My colleagues and I wanted to thank you—we call it "the last hooray," or "the second wind." I have myself observed this many times. Patients "come back" and die. I first witnessed this at nursing school. How confused I was, until an

older nurse told me that there were things that really characterized the daily experience of nursing, but that we wouldn't learn about in our normal training. How right she was!

I have read the article about your lecture and your work on the subject of terminal lucidity. In five years of working as a nurse, I witnessed terminal lucidity several times. A colleague of mine was the only person I could openly talk with about these experiences. I am glad and grateful that science has finally taken notice of this.

As a nun, I have been nursing and attending to our older sisters from the convent for years. We pray, we keep watch; we are there for our sisters. The first time I witnessed this was when our venerable Mother Superior Emeritus died. She had been suffering from advanced dementia for several years. But, for the last two days before her death, she came back to us. Her "old" self was restored, with all her spiritual and intellectual brilliance. She positively radiated. That was my first encounter with what you investigate. Our priest, however, had little use for any of this, and the physician in charge of our convent didn't hide the fact that he considered our report of the "revived Mother Superior" to be nothing more than a pious tale. Such a thing was impossible, he said, even if dementia patients did occasionally engage in behavior that resembled meaningful action—spontaneous healing was out of the question. And yet, our Mother Superior had recognized all eight of us sisters, recalled our names, as well as numerous details from the spiritual education she had given us. When, only a few years later, something very similar happened to our oldest sister at the convent, we didn't even try to talk to the doctor—he wasn't going to believe us anyway. I hope that this will change as a result of your and your colleagues' work.

"Can This Be Real?"

What also transpired from the letters I received was an aspect that receives scant attention, if any, in historical testimony—namely the reaction of family members who witnessed TL.

Many were deeply moved by and grateful for what they had experienced. It is not difficult to see why: between the diagnosis of a dementia disorder such as Alzheimer's and the death of the patient, some ten years on average will pass. These are ten years during which one painfully witnesses the steady erosion of the mental capacities, and soon the personality and character of the beloved person, head of the family, mother or grandmother, husband, good friend, uncle or aunt. Years of slow departure, and the fact that it is a slow departure doesn't make it any less painful—on the contrary. Finally, there comes a point when one realizes that caring for the relative at home, under one's own steam, has become nearly impossible—she will be admitted to a nursing home or, in the most advanced cases, to a hospice.

And then, one day comes the unexpected call: the nurse, or a relative, calls and reports that the patient is once again quite with it, that she is surprisingly well, memory returned, she recognizes her surroundings, speaks—that she expresses gratitude, maybe takes care of unfinished business, makes peace, is ready to take leave. One isn't sure what to think, but the urgency in the voice of the nurse or relative helps one to overcome any doubts: something very unusual is happening; something one doesn't want to miss. So one rushes to the nursing home and visits. And then, one witnesses the terminal lucidity of the person one had given up hoping to have a "normal conversation" with again—without understanding what is happening. How could one understand something there is no way to prepare for, something one in all likelihood hasn't even heard of? Returning home, bewildered, moved, one wonders. One hasn't expected such a thing to happen and starts to search for information, maybe online—and finds hardly anything.

Maybe one finds one's way to the discussion boards of hospice employees, or nurses working in palliative care units. These are the most likely venues for discussion on the subject, for the simple reason that this group is most likely to spend the most time with dying dementia patients and therefore to witness terminal lucidity. But such platforms rarely offer more than the odd personal account and some replies of those who also experienced it. There is no deeper validation for one's own experiences beyond that. This often creates a state of cognitive dissonance: on the one hand, one has just been witnessing and sharing a personal and deeply moving experience with one's dying spouse or relative or friend. Perhaps one realizes that this experience will have a profound impact on one's outlook on life and death and personhood (many told us that). The memory of it will remain with us. Yet on the other hand, there isn't even a word or definition for what one has just witnessed. Can it therefore be true? Can it be real? Another correspondent wrote:

> The "return" of my father was the only time in my life I have witnessed something akin to a medical miracle. However, when I started looking for people I could discuss this with, I soon realized that nothing makes one lonelier than the encounter with a miracle. No one I talked to had ever heard of this. Few were inclined to believe it in the first place. Others had never experienced anything like it, but immediately had some esoteric or paranormal explanation up their sleeve, which confused me even more and reinforced

my feeling of being alone with my experience. I wasn't looking for an explanation. I just wanted to talk to people who would listen to me and acknowledge my experience. But this wish was not granted.

When my boyfriend suffered from (AIDS-related) dementia, our friends were there for him until his behavior became unbearable to many of them. Their visits eventually tapered off. This was a terribly lonely time. The medication no longer worked. His confusion got worse by the day. Then, he went blind. Nothing remained of the erstwhile theater actor, who held so much promise in the eyes of his teachers—or rather: in the eyes of us all; who had been fabulous on stage, in the role of Cyrano de Bergerac; who always had an open heart for the unconventional and eccentric, for those who despaired of everyday normality. He had become a shadow of his former self; there was nothing remotely evocative of that amazing person. Only his beautiful hands remained, gesturing as he engaged in conversation with his hallucinations. Now he, who had never rejected anyone, had become an outcast. We were terribly lonely. In truth: I was terribly lonely. He, after all, had his imaginary companions. On his last day, however, shortly before he died, he looked me in the eyes. I swear: he was blind, but he somehow found my eyes and looked straight at me. He held my hand and thanked me for remaining with him to the last. Then he asked me to write down who of his friends and siblings should receive which books, as well as various mementos of his performances. He remembered. He was of course very weak and his speech was slow and his mouth dry. But beyond that he was quite revived, and as generous as ever. We spent some time rehearsing his ideas for his funeral. It was perfectly natural. And yet it was extraordinary—probably the most extraordinary experience of this entire arduous journey to his death. After roughly one or two hours, his powers left him. He had difficulties breathing and he dozed off. I quietly left the room and entered the hospital corridor. Leaving his sickbed was like leaving a magical space for the cold and brutal reality of the hospital.

When I met the ward physician in the corridor and told him that my boyfriend was completely lucid and conscious and had looked me in the eyes, he tersely commented that [his] blood values had deteriorated, that I should be prepared for the worst. When I telephoned some of our friends in the evening, I was met with near universal disbelief. I had been blessed, but do you know how lonely it is to be given a gift and having no one who even believes in it? My boyfriend died the next day, from a massive stroke. I was never happier, or more miserable, than those days. I keep this last encounter with my friend in my heart. I still can't speak or write about this without . . . crying, crying.

There are indeed few words that can describe what these people witness. There is almost no literature where one might learn what is at work here, or how others in similar situations have coped with it. But then again people—we—need stories and role models to deal with unusual or dramatic experiences: we need community. And the more complex, bewildering, and existential the phenomenon we face, the greater our longing for community, the greater our desire for validation, and the greater our need for support. If not in personal conversations, then at least in the shape of texts, narratives, and stories. But there is so little to draw on in this regard; in fact, this book is the first English-language book to extensively address the subject of terminal lucidity (the first book-length treatise on, among other things, terminal lucidity was written by Michael Nahm in German—*Wenn die Dunkelheit ein Ende findet*—and is highly recommended to readers who understand German). I hope more will follow.

At any rate, seen from this angle—the perspective and psychological needs of the witnesses—an additional approach to the issue thus presented itself, one that more closely resembles a psychotherapeutic or pastoral approach: one must also address the needs of those who are confronted with terminal lucidity and help them to find ways for how to come to terms, to cope with it. And this entails giving them the opportunity to relate their experience, to take them and their experience seriously, to acknowledge what and how they experienced it. To listen to their stories. This is true for everyone—and perhaps TL is a chance that we relearn to offer one another precisely what gives communities and established oral or written traditions such coherence and comfort: the possibility to bear witness to our experience—and to the manner in which we and others lived through it. Being listened to as well as listening gives us a sense of not being alone with our experiences—a sense of belonging—even if, or perhaps even especially if, we don't yet fully understand what we or others experienced. But we do need a forum for this—a community built around some of the most basic humane notions, such as a common language of appreciation, kindness, compassion, and mercy.

Against this backdrop, it may be less surprising that, in the first months after the publication of the reports on my work, so many people contacted me to share their experiences. However, what most moved me was the gratitude for taking them and their experience seriously and investigating the phenomenon systematically, as well as the great uncertainty that seemed to go hand in hand with the experience:

What we experienced as a family when we said goodbye to F was wonderful on the one hand, while profoundly confusing us on the other. There was, for example, the worry that we should have looked after F more when he was confused and apathetic. Had he been alert the entire time, and we just hadn't noticed? Had he wanted to communicate with us, and we were numb to it? And, if not—*where* had he been all that time? I must admit that all this unsettled me very much. This uncertainty sometimes offsets the joyful memory of the last lucid days with F. I know what I saw. I just cannot understand it.

What does one do about an experience one cannot possibly explain? In our family, we keep quiet about it, which has always been our way. It confused us, and each of us has worked through and banished the memory of my grandmother's lucid moments in his own way. We have hardly mentioned it since. My family prides itself on being rational, evaluating everything according to scientific criteria. This experience didn't fit our rational world, where everything is structured and always "clear"—except, that is, my grandmother's clarity of mind before she died. I think I am the only member of my family to try to understand all this, even falling back on some religious or spiritual approaches. Anyway—what I experienced with my grandmother somehow occupies a unique place in my family's worldview. That is probably why we usually keep quiet about it.

"Is It Time to Say Farewell?"

But uncertainty did and does continue, not only for the witnesses, but also for myself. I am periodically contacted by someone whose relative is at that very moment going through a lucid episode—and, since most cases discussed in the media tended to end in death within a few hours or days (*terminal* lucidity), those who contact me want to know whether the unexpected lucidity of their family member indicates his or her imminent passing. On several occasions I have been asked by a relative whether the lucid conversation with a patient was at the same time a farewell:

> My mother has suffered from dementia for the past ten years. It progressed very slowly in the beginning, but the last two years were awful. But she is going through this lucid time right now. Everybody is positively elated. It is a miracle. But what does it all mean? Is she going to die? Should we prepare for this?

> I found your article on terminal lucidity while trying to find more information on what is happening here. My grandfather's sister is, for the first time in months, perfectly responsive. Now we are worried she'll die very soon. Can you tell me what we can do to keep her with us a little longer? Or is it inevitable that she will now die?

> My mother has had dementia for six years and is now in the final stages. I have not had a conversation with her for a long, long time. When I went to visit her in the nursing home yesterday it was like I had my mum back again. I was utterly amazed as she started having a conversation with me and even called me by name, which she has not done for a few years. She recognized and spoke to family that she had not seen for a long time. Having read the article on terminal lucidity I thought I would let you know. I am of course wondering is she going to die very soon as according to the article this happens in dementia patients just before they die.

Imagine finding such an email in your inbox. You have no idea who wrote this to you; you do not know the person, their background, their age, nothing. And they ask you whether their mother, grandfather will die, and you try to be as comforting and helpful and honest as you can be toward someone who trusts you that much, though he or she does not even know you personally. So what do you say? How do you reply? Of course, I was neither able nor in fact willing to say what the prognosis of the respective patient was—and I am still unable and unwilling to do so now that, as a result of our research work, I can draw on a significantly larger case collection and have a somewhat better understanding of terminal lucidity. For there are cases, albeit rare in my database, of mere *paradoxical* lucidity: i.e., lucid episodes that resemble terminal lucidity in every respect—minus the fact that patients in terminal cases deteriorate and die within a short while after the episode, whereas paradoxical lucidity does not appear to be death-related. These cases are no less moving and no less bewildering.

One such case is the story of a patient who died a full two weeks after her lucid episode. The following report was written up by the hospice chaplain Ron Wooten-Green who had looked after the patient, an eighty-eight-year-old woman by the name of Liz, and her ninety-year-old husband, for several years.

Liz is an eighty-eight-year-old suffering the silent but ruthless ravages of Alzheimer's disease. It has been a long time since she has been able to connect with reality. She can have conversations; they just don't make a lot of sense. Luther, her faithful ninety-year-old husband, walks the two blocks to the nursing home three times a day to bring her flowers from the garden of their in-town home.

I have been visiting Liz and Luther for nearly a year now. I know what to expect. Whether he is there or not, Liz will be in her bed, and when I walk into her room she will glance toward the window and say, "That's a good ball game out there," referring to a small plot of grass with a crab apple tree in the middle—not a lot of room for a ball game. However, Liz seems to enjoy watching "them" play.

If Luther is there with her, she will be asking him: "Did you get the chores done? How are the cows doing? Did you get the milk? Now don't forget to feed the pigs. Bring me the eggs; I'll package them up." While they still own the farm outside of town, Luther has not farmed the land for nearly thirty years. He is renting the farm. They gave up raising hogs forty years ago. Liz has not candled an egg for nearly fifty years. But that's the way it is with Alzheimer's: the past is far more present than the present.

The doors open, but as I reach in to knock I notice an unusual scene. Liz is sitting in the wheelchair. In all this time I have never seen her out of bed. Luther is sitting on the edge of a comfortable overstuffed chair. His head is bowed. They are holding hands.

For a moment I am reconsidering whether I should break the spell of this couple enjoying each other's company. But just as I am about to turn on my heels and leave, Luther looks up, smiles, and greets me, ever welcoming, "Good to see you."

It is then that I notice that the cheery greeting betrays the tears glistening on his cheeks.

"I really do not wish to disturb you two. I can come back another time."

"No, no. You are not disturbing us. We were just sitting here."

"Now, Luther, it seems to me you were doing something more than just sitting here. I see tears. Want to tell me what's really going on? You certainly don't have to tell me. But I promise to listen, if it will help."

Liz, who is wearing her favorite sweatshirt with a pair of kittens embossed on the front, looks up at me without her trademark smile. "No one is playing ball. The ball game is over."

Liz appears troubled with a sadness I have never before seen.

"The ball game's over—that is for sure," Luther affirms. I smile at his comment, thinking that Luther is playing along with Liz, but I quickly take note that he is not smiling. He is dead serious.

"The ball game is over?" I repeat.

"We are going to lose the farm," Luther says, the agony in his voice reflecting deep despair.

As Luther is crying, Liz reaches over to take his hands. She pulls him forward and gently draws the grieving husband into her arms. Luther is sobbing now; Liz is crying softly. I stand amazed at the scene unfolding in front of me.

"Why?" Liz asks.

Luther looks up at his wife of nearly seventy years and explains, "In order to take care of you here."

"Why didn't you tell me?" Liz asks.

Startled and confused, Luther looks at me and then turns to Liz: "Because . . . because . . . well, I figured you wouldn't remember anyway."

And Liz, with the assurance that comes from having raised a family of six, coordinated untold numbers of community and church events, handled the finances of home and farm—this woman who has been unable to connect with the world around her for years now—tells the man of her life and love: "I know. But I need to know."

> Liz had no knowledge of this interchange the next day—
> the destructive dynamics of Alzheimer's resumed within
> seconds of that one clear moment her husband will never
> forget. [. . .] Liz died two weeks after the event. [. . .] Liz
> reconnected with the world around her and her troubled
> husband at a time when no one thought it was possible.[4]

Liz died a full two weeks after this very brief lucid episode. One occasionally hears such stories of what appear to be examples of paradoxical lucidity. As this phenomenon is even less studied than terminal lucidity, we know of no unique indicators to differentiate the two. In other words, there is currently no way of telling whether the unexpected lucid episode of a dementia patient is a precursor to his or her death. We don't know.

But we do know something much more relevant. For right there and then, when it happens, other questions than the prognosis of the patient may matter even more: Are we there—not just physically, but mentally, spiritually? Do we reach out? Can we listen? Are we ready and willing to be approachable by someone who has been "gone" for months or years and suddenly and unexpectedly "came back"? Regardless of the prognosis of the patient: those who witness TL have been bestowed with a gift, and so accepting it with gratitude and awareness seems to be an appropriate way of dealing with it, no matter for how long we can hold on to this gift. Embrace the bond that develops in this encounter, whether the other (or we) will be dying in a few hours, next week, or in forty years. This, then, is the only advice I could and can responsibly give when asked whether the unexpected lucidity of the family member or friend signifies the beginning of his or her last journey: seize the moment, honor and harness the moment of togetherness. It might be, but need not be, the last. Make good use of this moment to listen, to wish him or her well, to be generous and forgive. Others have done it. And they tell us that we do not have to understand everything in order to forgive. With terminal lucidity, there might not be enough time for that. You can try later, if you then still feel the need to understand. And be ready to accept that there'll be things we perhaps will never understand. But at this moment, when sharing what could be the last lucid moments with this family member or friend, should our lack of understanding really hinder us from participating in these moments of connection, heart-to-heart communication, and togetherness? And what about the good we shared or received from this person? Do we understand why he or she was so kind to us? Probably not—and if the one does not hinder us from sharing our gratitude, the other should not hinder us from forgiving in what might be a last chance of truly reaching out and relating to and with that person.

The only advice I could give to people who asked me for a prognosis therefore was to make the best of the situation—either the "return" of and reunion with the patient would be a wonderful and possibly even recurrent event, and thus an opportunity to meet one another with love more than once (the patient staying alive and permanently or intermittently lucid for some time). Or it would be the last conversation, and thus the last opportunity to say farewell to one another in peace, love, and dignity. In other words, the advice would have been the same in either case. If I've learned one thing from my work, it is that we cannot err by sharing too much kindness, connection, compassion, and togetherness when the opportunity arises (and it arises often). But we most often err when we refuse to share our kindness and benevolence.

What counts in such moments is not what separates but that which connects us. The light of connection and togetherness frequently shines in what, from the outside, look like very unlikely places. Death and dying can confront us with the tragic aspects of human existence—

with disease, vulnerability, frailty, and with suffering; but dying also confronts and reconnects us to our humanity. And so does, as we will see, TL.

To return to my correspondents' questions: in *all* but two such cases thus far, I received, usually within a few days, confirmation that the patient had indeed died; and I am glad to report that in most cases, these last encounters were indeed reunions of peace, of a "happy ending," a reconciliatory and grateful farewell:

> I have to give you some sad news: Grandmother peacefully passed away last night. So it was indeed terminal. It really wasn't just sad, but also wonderful. We sat with her the entire afternoon. My sister brought a family album and we looked at old photos. Wistfulness. Gratitude. Laughter. The nurse entered the room from time to time to look after us. She once came in when we all had tears in our eyes, as my grandmother contemplated her wedding pictures, saying how much she was looking forward to being reunited with my (late) grandfather. The next time the nurse came in was when we laughed at children's photos of me and my sister. Her third visit came when my grandmother had just fallen asleep after thanking each of us for all the good times before growing tired and reclining in her bed. All this happened within a few hours. I remained with her for a while as she slept, trying to make sense of this astounding afternoon. How beautiful and peaceful she looked! Visiting time came to an end. My grandmother died a few hours later, in her sleep. What a wonderful farewell!

What I anecdotally convey here also emerged from the first survey studies we conducted—and it was equally confirmed by the few studies on terminal lucidity that had previously been published. In Nahm and Greyson's case collection, the same pattern emerges: the majority of those who experienced an unexpected and spontaneous resurgence of their cognitive and verbal skills died within a time window of a few days from their lucid episode.

7

Casting Out the Nets

Going Deeper

After my first contact with some witnesses of contemporary TL episodes, I had gathered and systematically evaluated several additional contemporary cases,[1] and received a few dozen more unstructured reports in reaction to media reporting on our work. The next step, then, was to collect even more such cases, and to systematically look for structural differences and overlaps between them—still with the aim of gaining a deeper understanding of the phenomenology of TL. We therefore sent out another call for case reports—this time all over the world to a random selection of hospitals, hospices, and nursing homes, as well as to online groups and forums for (a) family members and friends of patients with dementias, (b) family members and friends of patients with other cognitively impairing neurological disorders (i.e., traumatic brain injury, etc.), (c) family members and friends of the chronically and terminally ill, (d) hospice workers and nurses, and (e) the healthcare professions in general.

The aim was no longer merely to find out whether the phenomenon actually occurred—the growing evidence by now indicated that it did indeed occur. It was now a matter of learning as much as possible about the phenomenon itself. Who experiences it? Are there demographic factors, such as gender or age, that show significant statistical relationships with the phenomenon? What was the patient's diagnosis? How long did the lucid interval last? Moreover, are there differences in occurrence and prevalence depending on the diagnosis of the patient? Could some specific circumstances in the days before, or on the day of, the episode have played a role in bringing about the lucid episode? For instance, we wondered whether the occurrence of terminal lucidity was particularly frequent at specific times of the day—it is common knowledge that, particularly among older people, cognitive performance is more closely aligned to circadian rhythms, so perhaps this was also a factor at play here? Or were there changes in medication?

A one-size-fits-all trigger or mechanism wasn't particularly likely to be at play in terminal lucidity, since it occurs in the course of a wide range of conditions; however, exactly because this phenomenon had not been systematically investigated, it seemed prudent to follow every conceivable lead, no matter how far-fetched, unlikely, or improbable. These might include any change in the patient's daily routine, possible certain foods or beverages, weather conditions, psychological factors such as visits from certain persons, or discussing certain subjects in the presence of the patient, among other potential factors.

The next question to address concerned the temporal relation of TL and the death of the patient. All hitherto collected data indicated that terminal lucidity was a specifically death-related phenomenon— but it is easy to imagine a number of settings in which the death-relatedness of TL could be apparent rather than real. It is possible, for example, that TL cases that preceded the death of the patient are more memorable than the odd unexpected lucid episode that was followed by a return to the pre-lucid cognitive impairment, thus leading to a kind of memory bias and overreporting of death-related cases.

So, was TL in fact death-related, or were there similarly dramatic lucid episodes in cases that didn't precede the patient's death? The abovementioned case of Liz, for instance, was a borderline case in more than one respect—after all, she lived another two weeks after what was a particularly short lucid interval. The timing of the lucid episode wouldn't necessarily have much bearing on the philosophical implications of the mind's dependence on the brain; the clinical question about whether a therapeutic approach can be derived from the causes of a lucid episode also is uncertain.[2]

As the term "terminal lucidity" suggests, in the majority of cases in my database, patients died between a few minutes to a couple of days after the lucid episode. In fact, all available studies—the historical works by Nahm and colleagues, the prospective study by Macleod the survey work by Fenwick, and a more recent Korean study[3]—seem to agree on this point, though only larger prospective studies with non-terminally ill or frail patients will tell us the whole story of paradoxical and terminal lucidity.

Beyond the primary characteristics, possible triggers, and the timing of terminal lucidity, I was also interested in what terminally lucid patients had to say during their lucid episode. What does someone who has been, sometimes for years, largely unresponsive, confused, and forgetful—but is suddenly "back"—talk about? What does someone who hasn't recognized his or her daughter, son, grandchildren, or spouse for months or years say to them once he or she again knows who they are? What do they say to their caregivers? What do they say about how they experienced themselves and the world when they were cognitively impaired? And was there some truth to the frequent anecdotal reports that a significant number of these patients hinted at, and a few clearly articulated that they would die soon after the episode?

And then there was the hitherto unresearched question of the psychological impact of witnessing such an episode on patients' family members, friends, and caretakers. I had by then received several reports and letters that lamented being left alone with their experience, but most family members felt that the "reawakening" of their ailing relative was a "gift." Most, but not all of them. Some were simply out of their depth, or shocked, and many more were bewildered. Against this backdrop, I felt that it was important to learn how family members and friends cope with the unexpected lucid episode of their relative. This question also had significant clinical relevance in terms of the support provided to relatives caring for dementia patients—a group of people, incidentally, that all too often escapes our attention, care, and support.

So, these were some of the questions waiting for an answer. In the following, I will try to answer them on the basis of both our survey data (i.e., the questionnaire study) and the case reports—"stories"—I receive on a regular basis.

A Caveat

The following is still only a preliminary step toward a better understanding of TL's phenomenology. I would not like to give the unjustified impression of having more certainty about TL than our data can support. More is needed. The people who contacted me (the majority of whom were not healthcare professionals, but family members or friends) were self-selected, meaning they chose, of their own accord, to share their case reports. The sample, therefore, may not be as representative of the general population as it ideally should or could be. While the following section moves us a little closer toward a better understanding of the phenomenology of TL, prospective study designs should provide us with additional reliable data on TL in the future.

{ 8 }

Witnesses

Who Experiences TL?

The first question we were interested in was: Are their specific markers or traits of individuals who experience an episode of terminal lucidity? Three simple differentiating criteria had to be taken into account: the gender of the patient, his or her age, and the diagnosis of the conditions presumed to be contributing or principal causes of the cognitive impairment of the patient before the lucid interval.

The question of the diagnosis was particularly significant because not all cognitively impairing disorders progress along the same patterns. For instance, patients suffering from Lewy body dementia (LBD) sometimes experience lucid intervals, especially in the early stages of the disease.[1] Seen from this angle, cases of terminal lucidity are perhaps not as clinically remarkable in early LBD patients as, for example, the return of a clear and alert consciousness, including memories and language skills, in patients suffering from advanced Alzheimer's or frontal-temporal dementia. In other disorders or conditions, such as cerebral abscesses, aftereffects of meningitis, strokes, brain tumors, and brain injuries, remission rates are low, albeit more variable. However, the *spontaneous* and *instantaneous* remissions so typical for TL have hardly been described outside the context of terminal lucidity, and patients suffering from these conditions usually require lengthy rehabilitation and training. Even then, progress in the recovery of functions is slow and rarely complete, but almost never spontaneous and instantaneous.

In our database, the most common diagnosis is dementia with no further specifier, followed by patients with Alzheimer's dementia, including a few cases with early-onset Alzheimer's dementia. The next largest group comprises vascular dementia and stroke patients, followed by patients with either primary or metastatic brain tumors, Parkinson's disease with dementia, Lewy body dementia, traumatic brain injury, Huntington's disease with cognitive decline/dementia and frontal-temporal dementia, HIV/AIDS–related dementia, and meningitis. A wide variety of medical conditions underlie the cognitive impairment of the patients who subsequently experienced TL, and there was also some variation in how confused or cognitive patients were:

My wife was mostly sleeping or unconscious, couldn't tell. But she rarely even opened her eyes.

He just stared—no specific fixation point. When food arrived, he would simply stare at the bread or apple, or at the water bottle in front of him. Didn't react when talked to.

The patient, an eighty-nine-year-old lady with advanced Alzheimer's, slipped in and out of sleep, but when awake, no communication was possible. She did not react when called by name. The only remote sign of reaction occurred when she heard the sound of running water when the cleaners were in her bathroom. But even that was brief, and there was no way of "connecting."

K had lost her memory over the years. When we told her about something, she beamed at us with her lovely pale blue eyes—I will never forget these beautiful eyes! This diminutive lady with the infinitely gentle face and personality she had preserved into her illness—she seemed almost transparent, her gentle smile was like a transparent glow. But, sadly—she listened amiably and attentively, yet forgot within seconds what we were saying. She occasionally reacted adequately, especially when we were talking about things in the distant past. However, as the disease progressed, such moments grew rare and she retreated into permanent silence. Only her smile remained. None of us could foresee how much this radiance would be rekindled once more when, in her gentle wisdom, she prepared us for her own death.

Over the years, D had become extremely forgetful and confused. She didn't always find her room and kept forgetting that she was no longer at home, but in a nursing home, a year after moving in. She tried, time and again, to call her late husband and confused her two children—and didn't recognize her grandchildren at all.

He was no longer able to master his daily life, so we hired a nursing care service that assisted him twice a day. Otherwise, he just sat in front of the television, watching his favorite series. I occasionally sat there with him. He clearly no longer really understood what he was watching. He sometimes commented on the show, but these comments confirmed that he was no longer able to follow the content. His behavior grew increasingly outlandish. He kept misplacing his wallet and searching the whole apartment (always very unsystematically). We regularly found things that clearly didn't belong there in the fridge or oven: his mobile phone, his glasses, etc. Unfortunately, his memory also deteriorated progressively. When I visited him, he recognized me on a good day. On a bad day, I had to introduce myself to him, which allowed him to make sense of who I was.

Her memory was like a sieve—it didn't retain anything for more than a day or two. She often felt overwhelmed as soon as the normal routine was somehow disrupted. Within her routine, however, she managed fairly well. But—woe betide if something unexpected happened: a marketing call could thoroughly unsettle her. Oh, and she loved shopping. And shop she did—she, who had always been quite frugal, was now on a shopping spree, and it wasn't always clear whether she had simply forgotten that she had already bought, say, a cooling fan, or a mysterious inspiration had somehow suggested that she needed more than one. The final score was no less than eight cooling fans. She was nonetheless still able to live in her own apartment.

Next to patients with neurological disorders, there is yet another group of medical conditions in which TL has been observed. These severe psychiatric disorders, such as psychoses, form a separate group. While the latter can be non-responsive to therapy, especially once they have become chronic, an episodic course of psychiatric disorders with lucid intervals is not completely out of the ordinary. Because significant variations in the course of psychoses are a defining feature of these disorders' general pathology, and larger *structural* changes in the brain are not consistently observed in this patient group, we decided not to further pursue such cases for this study. Nonetheless, individual case histories involving terminal lucidity in chronic psychotic patients do occasionally appear in literature—such as the early Russian report by Turetskaia and Romanenko (1975) describing three patients who had been in psychiatric inpatient care for eleven, twenty, and twenty-seven years, respectively. All three patients "awoke" shortly before their death and were cognitively clear and coherent during their terminal lucid episodes.[2] In our case collection, we also have a number of comparable instances that, for the reasons given above, are not described in the following section.

Additionally, only diagnoses in which severe cognitive impairment is part of the clinical picture were included. A number of case reports referred to other diagnoses—such as cancer (other than brain), COPD, liver failure, multiple organ failure, sepsis, etc., but these cases, too, are not included in the following, because—similarly to the psychoses—a waxing and waning of cognitive impairment is a regular, or at least occasional, feature of these ailments.

Age and Gender

In view of the fact that cognitive impairment is significantly related to advancing age, it is not surprising to find a preponderance of patients aged sixty-five and older. Nonetheless, there is a wide range of patients' ages, varying between eight and one hundred years; the youngest patient (a girl suffering from an inoperable brain tumor [grade III astrocytoma]) was eight years old, the oldest patient (Alzheimer's) was one hundred years old. Some 20 percent of patients were younger than sixty-five. This ratio of age groups is mirrored by the gender ratio—women in most industrialized nations have a higher life expectancy than men and thus also a higher dementia risk, and we, too, have slightly more reports about female patients than about male patients.

Length of Episode

The next question concerns the length of the lucid episode. It varied considerably: most episodes lasted between ten minutes and several hours, and only about a tenth of cases lasted either less than ten minutes or more than a full day. However, several respondents said that they weren't sure how long the lucid episode really lasted—either because they arrived by the patient's side after the episode had commenced, or because they were so emotionally involved (or confused) that they had lost track of time.

Cognitive State During Lucid Episode

The next question concerns the patient's cognitive state during the lucid episode. On the basis of our case collection (as well as earlier case reports), we soon saw that not all TL episodes look the same. In some cases, the patient makes what only can be called "a full return"; in others, however, the patient may appear to be clear and lucid, but witnesses were not entirely sure how coherent he or she was. In yet another class of cases, the patient seems to be clear and lucid, yet his verbal communications are largely incoherent. And in a relatively small group, the patient seemed lucid, but no verbal communication took place. There are thus four rough categories of terminal lucidity:

1. clear, coherent, and "just about normal" verbal communication;
2. clear and lucid, but informant was not totally sure about coherence of verbal communications;
3. clear and lucid, but largely incoherent in verbal communications;

4. clear and apparently lucid, but nonverbal communica-
    tion (gestures, gaze, etc.).

In our case collection, 78 percent of the patients were "clear, coherent, and just about normal verbal communication" during their lucid
episode (category 1), and 8 percent seemed "clear and lucid, but there
remained some uncertainty as to the coherence of their verbal communications" (category 2). A very small group—3 percent—seemed
"lucid, but their verbal communications were clearly incoherent"
(category 3), and in 11 percent of cases, the patients were clear and
apparently lucid, but no verbal communication took place (category
4). Strikingly then, nearly 80 percent of patients didn't merely show a
slight improvement in their general condition, but experienced a full
recovery of their memories and verbal skills—in short, their entire
former personality and abilities had come back. These results seem to
echo many of the earlier findings and reports discussed above.

However, it is important to note that only prospective studies will
allow us to come to more certain conclusions of the degree of cognitive
clarity and coherence during a TL episode. There are several reasons
why TL episodes with dramatic, full-blown returns of cognitive and
verbal ability may be overreported and those that are less dramatic
might go underreported. For instance, witnesses may have been more
eager and motivated to share information about clear-cut and unam-
biguous cases of TL, and others might have been less motivated to
report episodes of categories 2 through 4 as they didn't fit the then-
spreading common narrative of TL as signifying a full return of mental ability. It is also possible that those who witnessed such episodes
were uncertain whether a category 2, 3, or 4 episode did qualify at all
for what we were looking for, and therefore refrained from reporting
such cases. Occasionally, case reports on categories 2 through 4 came
with a note that respondents were unsure whether their report would
be eligible at all: "I am not sure whether this is what you are looking

for"; "I hope you can also address cases such as ours, even if it does not fully match the description." On the other hand, respondents reporting category 1 cases usually displayed high confidence that their case report matched criteria. Clearly then, there are several sources of potential bias and the proportions of categories 1, 2, 3, and 4 we find in our case collection may not necessarily represent the true relative number of category 1 through 4 cases. These data therefore still await confirmation from more studies and case reports being collected under better controlled conditions.

So much for the sheer numbers and their remaining uncertainties. But as I said, these numbers obviously don't come even close to the full picture of what really happened in these episodes:

Category 1:

My mother was the center of our family. She was my warm and loving mother, but as her dementia progressed, she became increasingly aloof, cold, absent. It was very painful to watch her transfomation. I will never forget the day when she no longer recognized me and I had to introduce myself to her. It was so incredibly painful. Here was my mother, and yet, she was no more. On her last day, however, everything was different. When I entered the room, she looked at me and called out my name. She recognized me. She radiated the very motherly love I had missed for so many months after that fateful day when she no longer recognized me. But now, she did, and when I started to cry, she said, "No, no. That is not the way. Come here!" I sat down next to her, and she took my hand and we had the most wonderful last conversation. We talked about my childhood, my daughters, my plans for our new house, about her illness. I had my mother back, and I relished every moment, drinking in her motherly energy and kindness. It was simply wonderful. [...] After an hour, she said that she was tired. She looked at me, literally pouring out her love. Everything was good. Everything was right. Everything that needed to be said had been said. Now there was only motherly love and my love for her. I knew somehow intuitively that this would not last. But with this farewell, even if it was painful, I was okay. I had my mother back and I was ready for whatever was to come now. She then slowly shook her head and then softly nodded. I nodded, too, and then she closed her eyes. I left the room and as soon as I closed the door, I broke out in tears, both of joy and of sadness. I somehow knew that this would be our last time together. She died the same evening.

The following case also qualifies for category 1—in other words, full remission. Moreover, the patient in this case history demonstrated not just a reawakening of her former personality, but an increased overall vitality and zest for life. Almost a quarter of TL witnesses reported such increased energy and elation:

My mother died on Monday evening; the day of the eclipse. She'd had Alzheimer's since 2011 and had been in the care home for over a year. I'd visited her at least every Sunday since she'd been in the nursing home and had watched her deterioration, especially over the last month, knowing that she didn't have much time left. She was silent and unresponsive. Long past the stage of not recognizing us and no eye contact; she'd even stopped saying "No" to everything. [. . .]

On Mum's last Sunday, I was with my two daughters and as we came into view she recognized us and greeted us with joy. She talked with us as we combed and plaited her hair. One of my daughters took pictures of her hair and showed it to her and she said it looked beautiful. Then she fell asleep and we kissed her goodbye and left.

Staff at the care home said that she'd been fine the next day. Laughing and chatting. The daughter of one of the other residents had given her a cake, just before Mum had danced back to her room, for her personal care. She'd used the toilet and was chatting with them happily, when she slumped to the side and breathed her last. They thought she'd fainted and fanned her at first, before realizing that she'd stopped breathing and called the paramedics.

They fought for an hour to bring my mum back. When my son and daughters arrived, they told my son the paramedics detected a pulse and continued to try and resuscitate her. They couldn't bring her back though and eventually pronounced her dead.

The following case describes a similar revival; it was sent to me by the patient's consulting physician:

I am a retired palliative care physician and witnessed or was told about many examples of TL during my twenty-five years of practice. The most striking was a sixty-year-old woman dying as a result of metastatic brain cancer. She was cared for at home by her family and was ably supported by the general practitioner [GP] and community nurses. She ultimately became unresponsive and unconscious. An indwelling urinary catheter was inserted and a subcutaneous infusion of morphine and midazolam was instituted.

Because she was comfortable I arranged for her GP to supervise this lady's ongoing care and promised the family I would ring each morning. On the first two mornings I was told that she was peaceful and had not stirred, opened her eyes, or given any sign that she was conscious.

On the third morning I was told she was sitting up in the kitchen drinking champagne! My stunned silence was noted by the daughter who said, "Oh, Doctor, you aren't aware but today is my mother's birthday and she is sitting up with all the family and partying." This lady went to bed later that morning lapsed back into her "unconscious" state and died twenty-four hours later.

One person—the only one so far in my case collection—witnessed TL in both her father and mother, who died about one year apart:

My father passed first. The hospital staff had become very close to my dad as he was in and out a lot. When my dad (who was semiconscious at the time) let me know he didn't want any further medical assistance, the staff moved him to a beautiful private room. He no longer communicated and was slipping away. My uncle rushed in from NYC to see him before he passed. When my dad heard his voice, he opened his eyes and tried to sit up. I was shocked. They talked for about twenty minutes about boats and my dad charting a course for the fall, and then my dad said he was a little tired. We left for a quick dinner. Upon my return, I sat by my dad's side and told him about dinner and how happy my uncle was to have seen him. I was surprised by his alertness. We held hands and I told him about a Western that was on the TV. He said it was late and he'd watch TV tomorrow.

He told me to go to sleep (I was living in the room with him). I laid on my bed watching him and the TV. He would catch me and tell me to get rest. I don't remember, but I fell asleep and woke up a few hours later . . . he was gone. He had to have been awake for about four hours.

One year later my mom had lost all understandable speech (word salad/jumble). She had to be admitted to the hospital for an upper respiratory infection. After she was there two days, the hospital staff suggested I place her back on DNR and prepare myself. I called my family (most from NY) and told them to make arrangements to come see her. They came two days later. I told her they were coming and while she would smile or squeeze my hand when I spoke, she was bedridden with her eyes closed. The Sunday had come and her family was on their way. When I got to the hospital, she spoke to me. She asked me to help her into the bathroom to color and wash her hair! I was stunned. My daughter got hair color and we quickly took care of all of her beauty needs. We got her back in bed and she asked for lipstick. No oxygen. My daughter, my aunt who had helped me with her at home, and I kept making faces at each other in confusion. How was this possible? The family came for about two hours. She ate. She sang with them. She exchanged stories. She asked about their lives. They all stared at me as if I was crazy! My uncle told the aunt who was helping me that she and I needed a vacation and he would hire a nurse because my mom was fine . . . and she was. I walked them all to the elevator and by the time I got back she was not really making sense again. She was frowning which usually meant pain, so the nurse gave her some medication. My aunt called the room to see how it was going and I told her. She was so confused. As we spoke, my mom opened her eyes, squeezed my hand, and said, "my poor baby." That was it. She was gone. I was shocked! What the heck happened? We were all so confused by the events of that day. When I called my uncle to tell him, he was devastated.

I tell you these two stories so that you know that you are on to something very real. Both times the staff told me how common it was. They referred to it as "rallying."

Some witnesses also reported visible changes to the patient's appearance:

During his lucid episode, my dad (age 75) looked ten to fifteen years younger, coloring perfect and his eyes that had been milky for the last few years were crystal blue once again and twinkling as he looked at me—the way I remember him from years before.

My eighty-three-year-old mother suffered from severe Alzheimer's disease and passed away on January 10. She was diagnosed almost five years ago, and until the five days before her death, my mother's quality of life was extremely poor. She slept or dozed up to twenty hours a day and aside from eating, needed assistance with all aspects of daily living.

On January 5, she "complained" that her chest hurt and we took her to the hospital where we were informed she had suffered a mild heart attack. Once we arrived at the hospital, she said she felt no more pain and while in the ER, we had the great pleasure of discovering that my mother had regained her cognition, verbal, and bathroom skills. During the next three and a half days that she spent in the hospital, she was like her old self. She delighted everyone in the hospital. The nurses on the floor said unless we told them she had Alzheimer's, they would have just thought she was an elderly woman with a cardiac condition. She also regained much of her energy, and performed an extraordinary occupational therapy exercise session the day after her attack.

She asked questions and understood everything. She expressed concern for her family members. She hugged and kissed us. She critiqued the hospital decor. She took a walk with me on the hospital floor and encouraged me to let her walk more. She spoke on the phone with friends and relatives who were ecstatic that my mother had "returned." She read and commented on articles in *The New York Times*.

She exhibited her sense of humor and joked with us. She was released from the hospital on January 9 and upon arriving home, walked into rooms that she hadn't been in for the past five years. She looked around and said with a smile, "The house still looks good." When I asked her about her prior condition over the past few years she replied, "I don't remember that." She suffered a second small heart attack on the evening of January 9 and passed away at home the next night. She was uncomfortable, but completely lucid until the end.

Not Alone in Death

But what about the cases in which respondents said that they were unsure whether the patient's utterances were coherent (category 2), or in which they were quite certain that the patient's communication was entirely incoherent (category 3)? These categories merit closer scrutiny, as they occasionally confront us with some tenacious problems pertaining to interpretation and categorization of coherence and lucidity under very uncommon circumstances. Generally, the reports in this category suggested that the patient's state couldn't generally be classified among the usual criteria of cognitive incoherence in the dying process—i.e., terminal delirium or hallucinations; certainly not without lingering doubts. The respondents frequently expressed such doubts themselves.

In the majority of cases in category 2, in other words: witnesses weren't sure whether the patients were coherent, or to what extent their utterances were coherent; the patients spoke about—or with—absent, mostly dead persons:

My dad was in a nursing home for half a year. He had severe dementia and could no longer formulate a sentence. He didn't recognize us.

On the day he died, however, he knew exactly who I was. He looked at me and starting speaking! He said that he knew that he would not be much longer in this home. I was not sure what he meant or whether he was "healed" and wanted to move to his flat again. But he shook his head. "Last night, David came and said he would take me home." David was his older brother. He had died four weeks before. We had told my dad once, but never mentioned it again as we were sure that he had not understood. When dad talked about his beloved David, I bit my lips so that I didn't cry right there and then. But dad looked so happy, so joyous! He really looked forward to leaving the nursing home. Dad died that very night.

My sister Monica was dying from an aggressive brain tumor. It progressed very fast, and during her last weeks, she was barely conscious. When the doctors informed us that her health had declined and that she'd entered the final stage, my wife and I visited her every day. On this day, we brought fresh flowers to her room. Monica had been asleep (she slept most of the time during these last days). But suddenly, Monica sat up in the hospital bed, looked at us, and then stared at the foot of the bed and in a loud voice said, "Liz!" Liz was her best friend. She had died four years before (breast cancer). Monica looked very peaceful. Gone was the sad stare, the tired and pain-stricken look in her eyes. She then tried to say something, but was too weak. But she looked so relaxed, so peaceful, so normal and healthy. Monica died a few hours later that night. I am still not sure what to make of this experience. Sometimes, I really believe that Liz had come to help Monica on her final journey. Sometimes, I wonder if she was hallucinating. But then, she so much changed after the brief "encounter" with Liz. So peaceful, so normal. It was as if she was back with us and at the same time was moving on to another plane. I still do not know what to make of it. But I am simply grateful that my sister had such a peaceful death after all the pain and fear she had to go through after her diagnosis.

My dad had dementia for many years. It started very slowly, but his last year, he was extremely impaired. I visited him very often, almost every two or three days. On his last afternoon, he opened his eyes and smiled at me, said hello, and asked me how I was. He was smiling and looked very happy. Then he said: "Mum is coming. We love you!" Mum had died two years ago. I wondered whether my father was hallucinating. But he was so clear. His eyes had cleared, he knew my name, his speech was fast and normal. I did not know what to say and he looked at me and smiled, as if to say: "It's okay. I love you." My father and I were silent for some minutes, then he slipped back into unconsciousness. He died a few hours later.

As my father breathed his last, he suddenly opened his eyes and asked: "Did you see that? This is breathtakingly beautiful! Wow!" Without sounding too woo-woo, I am certain what we saw was his soul departing that worn-out meat suit, finally free.

What are we to do with these cases? Clearly, these are not the usually chaotic, often frightening, hallucinations or delirious states that can occasionally occur in terminal delirium. We in fact found no such case in our database. Rather, these patients did unquestionably experience a return of their verbal skills, they unquestionably recovered memories of others—memories that had been inaccessible to them for a long time before they entered into an episode of terminal lucidity, yet they additionally experienced, saw, or heard things that those around them did not. While under normal circumstances, this is precisely what constitutes hallucinations, the primary feature of these episodes still was lucidity rather than confusion: the patients were alert, at least to the extent that they were often aware of the fact that their life was coming to an end, and they sometimes took the opportunity to bid farewell to those around them, entering into verbal communication with them.

Perhaps we might therefore describe these cases as belonging to a hybrid type—on the one hand, they unquestionably experienced a lucid interval, while on the other hand there were elements in their experience that no longer corresponded to the shared, objective reality of the hospital or nursing home room. The latter elements are consistent with the end-of-life experiences studied in recent years by other researchers such as the British neurophysiologist Peter Fenwick, whose research group reported "visitation experiences" among a number of dying patients not suffering from dementia or related neurological disorders.[3] It is perhaps not surprising, then, that we would occasionally find such cases among our TL patients.

It can be rather difficult to decide whether to interpret such cases as mere hallucinations and terminal deliria—especially since terminal delirium doesn't tend to be associated with the peaceful and positive emotions that are reported in the vast majority of these cases. Additionally, I have yet to come across cases in this category where, instead of relating visions of deceased relatives or religious themes, patients describe entirely nonsensical experiential visions or hallucinations of living persons. Hence, in view of their somewhat peculiar profile, it might be prudent to just let these reports stand for now, without prematurely writing all of them off as mere hallucinations or delusions.

"But Can't You Hear This Beautiful Music?"

So what to do with them? Here's a lesson from history that I believe sums up how we might regard them for the moment: When the Russian composer Sergei Rachmaninoff was on his last concert tour through the United States, he unexpectedly fell severely ill. He had to cancel his tour and was taken to his house in Beverly Hills, the very house of that he had recently foretold would be his last house in this world: "This is where I will die."

In the evening of March 28, 1943, Rachmaninoff was on his deathbed. His breathing slowed down, he became calmer, he closed his eyes . . . but then, he suddenly opened his eyes again and looked positively elated. He heard music. His last music. And he tried to persuade those around him that music was being played somewhere close by. But nobody else heard anything. Everyone else in the room insisted that no music was being played; it was quiet in Rachmaninoff's death chamber. Rachmaninoff eventually gave in: "Then the music is in my head." He lay back on his pillow and died shortly thereafter.[4]

Hallucinations? Incoherent? Delusional? Maybe, but does it matter? And how can we possibly know, as nobody asked Rachmaninoff what he had heard? Wasn't the insistence on silence, on the absence of music, a wasted opportunity? Why did no one ask Rachmaninoff what music *he* was hearing, instead of insisting that there was no music? For whatever Rachmaninoff heard, and wherever that tune came from, it was the last music one of the greatest Russian composers of the last century was ever going to hear in his lifetime. So those around him missed the opportunity to tune in to the reality of the last music of a great composer; and who is to say that it was anything less than real—if only *for him*? How, then, are we supposed to interpret cases where the dying, in their lucid episode, perceive things that others fail to perceive? I must admit that after hearing several such stories—from very believable sources at that—I no longer know. And I must admit that there *was* a time—namely at the beginning of my research—when I prematurely thought that these were "all hallucinations." Today, I believe that the most honest answer we can give is: we just don't know what these visions signify; what they mean; what these people actually do see or hear.

But as mentioned earlier, we know from the work of other research groups that such phenomena are not rare at all among the dying. And we know, if not how to interpret such occurrences, at least how to react to them, how to act: by trying to maintain communication, by listening, by being supportive, by being receptive to the stories people tell us. By being there. And that means, above all: not assuming that *our* view of reality is the only valid perspective. For the moment of dying may be many things—but it is no time for claiming to know it all, when we certainly do not.

The effort required to deny the (subjective or objective) reality of the last moments in the life of a dying person would be put to more productive and honest use if we took the opportunity to enter, together with the dying, the calm and peaceful space that can unfold around those last moments. I owe this lesson to a colleague who works in a hospice.

She, too, observes that her dying patients occasionally speak with or about individuals who had "come to meet them," but who nobody else can see or hear. "Can you see them? Can you hear them talking to me?" they ask. And this hospice nurse answers, with the greatest possible honesty, acknowledging the inner world of the dying: "No, I cannot see them at this moment, and I cannot hear what they say. But that is not so important. Would you like to talk about the people who visit you and what they tell you?" This nurse's reply may be even more accurate than if she insisted that "nobody is here." Leave it at that.

Next, there was a relatively small group where those present were quite sure that what the patients were saying was not coherent at all. From the reports, it seems as if most of these patients were obviously hallucinating—one patient, for instance, believed that a large oak tree had grown in her room overnight; another insisted on wearing new boots (she was barefoot in bed) and wasn't sure whether she liked wearing them, but now that she had them, thought she might as well go for a walk. It is tempting to interpret at least some of these communications as deeply symbolic—several respondents, particularly hospice personnel, hold the view:

> When a dying person speaks in symbolic language, the moment can be a challenging one for loved ones or healthcare workers. The words can evoke feelings of fear, impatience, and/or bewilderment for those standing at the bedside. What is important to remember, however, is that within those seemingly enigmatic words is a specific intent, a message to others from the patient's nearing death awareness (NDA). If [. . .] words from bedridden patients with terminal illness are taken literally, they seem like the hallucinatory ramblings of deteriorating minds. Often, NDA symptoms are attributed to other clinical situations such as delirium, side effects of medication, or psychiatric illness. [. . .] But those vocally exhibiting NDA behavior will usually present themselves with themes of strong intent, specifically in the form of metaphorical language. Unfortunately, many times

the response is to ignore, argue with him/her, make a joke of the comments, or provide medication to relax the patient. [...] But if one examines the language in a symbolic sense rather than straightforwardly, those nearby can become more aware of the specific desires and needs of the patient, as well as gain greater knowledge of what the death experience actually feels like.[5]

Does this also apply to at least some of our cases where the classification "clear and lucid, but largely incoherent in verbal communications" was selected? Once again, it may be premature to claim to know more than we do. At best we can say: if the symbolic language describing a different reality (or the same reality, described with different words and images) lies within the spectrum of "normal dying," encountering it from time to time in the context of terminal lucidity shouldn't come as a surprise. In any case, the group of patients deemed incoherent is currently so small (3 percent of the entire sample) that more such cases would be needed for a detailed analysis, based on which we might come to more reliable conclusions.

Holding Their Hands

Finally, there was a group about which respondents reported that they had the clear impression that patients were lucid, but no verbal communication took place. In some of these cases, the lack of verbal communication might have been a result of physiological conditions (such as facial paralysis resulting from stroke, or an oxygen mask). In a number of cases, however, the respondents had the clear impression that *meaningful* nonverbal communication with the patient had occurred, though it often was difficult to decide from the available descriptions whether the eye contact, say, or the holding and squeezing of a hand, or stroking of the back of the hand represent terminal lucidity in each and every one of these cases.

It again seems prudent to let these cases stand as valid for the time being, and to refrain from further interpretation until we are able to apply better and more accurate criteria for the evaluation and assessment of terminal lucidity and its possible manifestations. More important, we should refrain until we have a greater number of cases of terminal lucidity with nonverbal communication at our disposal for further investigation and analysis. For example, here is an account of nonverbal, seemingly reactive communication from my case collection:

My mother was a very "physical" person, who often hugged us when we were children, took us by the hand, or linked arms with us. She was kindness and warmth personified. However, in the course of her progressive illness, she grew increasingly "absent," maybe even aloof, and no longer enjoyed being touched. Whenever I wanted, by force of habit, to take her hand, she removed it and muttered something that was meant to convey that it made her uncomfortable— at least that's what it usually sounded like. I missed this personal exchange all the more as she grew increasingly silent in the last months of her life. She remained silent, was unresponsive, didn't even react when one called her name. However, in the last two days of her life, things changed: I clearly remember sitting next to her bed, and how she suddenly took my hand. I was unable in this moment to hold back my tears. And she looked at me, placed her second hand on my forearm. We remained in this position for what seemed like an eternity—and I indulged in her touch. My sister had a similar experience the following day. My mother took her hand and my sister was equally moved, whereupon my mother squeezed her hand more firmly. In that way, we had a farewell that, while hardly comprehensible to others, was deeply meaningful and "typical" for us.

The Last Conversation

The next question to explore is what the patients talked about—if indeed they communicated verbally. Further analysis of these reports shows a result I hadn't initially anticipated: many indicated that the patient was aware that he or she had been in a cognitively impaired state before the lucid episode, and that a significant number of patients seemed to know that their lucid time window was not going to last. Some even spoke explicitly about their impending death and used the remaining time to bid farewell to their family, friends, and caregivers. These findings, incidentally, again coincide with the results obtained by the research group around Peter Fenwick, and also showed that a large number of patients who were part of this study had accurate forebodings of their impending death.

Altogether, there were five recurring conversation topics reported: reminiscing with family members; awareness of impending death; preparations and last wishes ("unfinished business"); and, occasionally, bodily concerns (such as hunger or thirst). In the majority of cases, more than one of these topics was discussed during the lucid episode:

> Had a wonderful conversation. Talked about her last wishes. About family members. Told us that we should not argue with one another and respect her wishes. Talked about each of her children and their future. It was all very clear and urgent.

> My mother said that she felt so much better (in fact she had severe dementia for months and did not speak for the last month). She wanted to sit by the open window (it was a

beautiful summer) and she asked for chocolate! I went to the vending machine in the entrance hall and bought her favorite chocolate. She devoured it with intense joy. I think I never saw someone celebrating her chocolate as she did.

My father and I spoke for more than an hour. We remembered old times—his memories were very clear and he remembered the names of several places I had long forgotten. Then he spoke about things and objects that were not included in his testament and that he wanted to divide among his family and friends. He remained very calm and serene throughout that time, very controlled and clear. With hindsight, I would say that in his mind he had already taken leave from this world and just wanted to make sure he left it in good order. At the end he spoke about his funeral and its organization. It was something special, but he held this conversation in such a calm and relaxed manner, with such a sense of responsibility, that what had just happened only dawned on me on my way home, as I sat in the car: my father had said goodbye in his own way. The farewell he had prepared was so unexpected and clear that I only felt deep, deep grief after the funeral. This person—paragon of a mature, loving, and responsible person—had now gone forever. I miss him more than ever, day after day. It was the kind of farewell only he could think of.

My grandfather had advanced dementia. When the nursing staff told us that his health declined and that there was little they could do, I began visiting him more frequently. I often sat next to his bed and told him I was there, not sure whether he understood me at all. One day, however—it turned out to be his last day—I was totally shocked when he greeted me and inquired about the family, especially about his sister who also had advanced dementia. When I told him that we were supporting her in so many ways and that she was forgetful, but peaceful and happy, he was very relieved. He looked very peaceful and relaxed. He thanked me and said, "Tell her I love her. I will be waiting for her." Shortly thereafter, he fell asleep. He died a few hours later.

My grandfather then became very concerned to bring everything in order. He asked me to return some expensive art books to a colleague from whom he had borrowed them months ago when he was already impaired, but still liked looking at paintings. He said that we should give some of his books to this colleague if we did not want to keep them. Then he asked whether there was anything we wanted to tell him or whether we had any questions. We were really surprised and did not know what to say. My grandfather looked very satisfied and then said that he felt that everything was in order and how nice that was. He looked very relaxed, even playful after that. [The patient died the next morning].

The patient was in palliative care for dementia. He had severe cognitive decline over the preceding four months, no recognition of family or friends, paranoia, hallucinations, confusion, social withdrawal, refusal of food and drink, mumbling incoherent speech, lack of ability to toilet or shower himself, etc. He spoke for approximately twenty minutes and was able to inquire about family and friends that he previously could not recognize or remember. He had no recollection of the previous days' activities but mentioned that he had been in a mental fog for "the past few weeks" (it had actually been almost four months). He spoke to myself (granddaughter) as well as his wife and daughters. He asked to pass on messages to family members and spoke of specific details about them such as recalling favorite memories. Two weeks before, he was unable to recognize these persons on the phone and could not hold a conversation with them. He said he wished his death would come quicker. After twenty minutes he became tired and fell asleep/unconscious. He did not rouse or speak again and died shortly afterward.

As my grandmother lay in her deathbed, my grandfather sat beside her. The two of them had been married for more than sixty years and now this loving husband sat next to her sickbed, shaking with grief. He was also confused, because she had for the first time recognized him that day, and deeply saddened because the doctors were telling us that my grandmother was dying. Tears ran down their cheeks and even the nurse, who occasionally entered the room quietly to check on us, struggled to hold back her tears. My grandfather said: "I love you," sobbing uncontrollably. My grandmother looked at him and said something wonderful: "Take care of our garden as a sign of our love." My grandparents had a beautiful little garden, which my grandmother always lovingly tended, as long as she was able to. My grandfather sat in the garden on warm summer months and read to her from the newspaper, or the two of them talked while she did her gardening. The garden thus meant a lot to them. And her good advice to my grandfather to channel his love and grief for her into the garden was indeed going to work miracles. My grandfather truly came into bloom, just like the garden he tended.

As these reports show, there was a wide range of communication content—just as one would expect under less dramatic circumstances, when conversations are recorded. Moreover, a considerable number of our study participants confirmed that the manner in which the patients communicated mirrored their pre-morbid communication style.

In conclusion: as to the conversational topics during the lucid episode, next to references to bodily concerns (such as hunger or thirst), our findings again echo Macleod's 2009 observation that terminal lucidity "can provide an opportunity to 'set one's house in order,' offer a deathbed speech, and bid farewell."[6] The majority of the patients for whom information about conversational topics during the lucid episode was provided did just that, and accordingly, the episode was generally remembered as a "rewarding experience" by most of the survey respondents. But not by all, as we will see later.

Proximity to Patient's Death

As mentioned above, there remains the question whether unexpected lucid episodes represent a uniquely death-related phenomenon ("terminal lucidity"), or rather designate remarkable cases of transient cognitive fluctuations that only after the death of the patient are retrospectively attributed, or brought into connection, with his or her death.

In our case collection, about a third of the patients died within less than two hours after the lucid episode; another third died within two hours and a day; and a fifth died within two or three days; whereas in less than 10 percent of cases, the patient died within four to seven days, and in about 5 percent, the patient died after more than eight days, or not at all near the lucid episode. Hence in our sample, lucid episodes were indeed strongly death-related: over 90 percent died within days or hours.

As I already pointed out, the strong association between lucid episodes and imminent death that we found in our study still needs to be interpreted cautiously. By the time we received most case reports, my research interest in *terminal* lucidity was already widely known, most likely also among some of the respondents, some of whom were recruited from internet groups in which earlier reports about our *terminal* lucidity work had been discussed previously. In an ideal scenario, you would prefer to have study participants who do not know what you are looking for; you want what is called a "naive sample," which simply reports what they experienced or saw, and not what they believe you may want to hear.

On the other hand, as an approximate control for this factor, we can compare these results with the data obtained *before* our work was better known—our pilot study. Though this is only a rough test, it is still quite reassuring to see that the rate of cases of lucid episodes in close temporal proximity to the death of the patient did not differ significantly as a function of the recruitment time: the rate of non-terminal, i.e., merely paradoxical, lucidity cases amounted to roughly 5 percent of the sample of respondents recruited for the pilot study (i.e., before the media reported on our work), and 5 percent among the more recent cases.

Furthermore, the historical data from Nahm and Greyson's review are also in the same ballpark: in their sample of forty-nine cases, many with dementia, 43 percent of TL episodes occurred within the last day of life; 41 percent within two to seven days before death; and 10 percent within eight to thirty days before death. And in a recent Korean study by Lim et al., 50 percent died within a week and 50 percent died within nine days, though few of these patients had diagnosed neurodegenerative issues, so it is not quite clear how their findings can be compared to those reported here. If, therefore, we cannot completely rule out a certain response bias, earlier comparative data suggest that this effect, assuming it had any impact at all, did not significantly skew results.

Acknowledging the uncertainties that require more data and cases, the existing data thus support the existence of a death-related return of cognitive function and communication ability in patients whose diagnosis renders such a return unlikely.

Triggers and Causes

One striking feature of TL is how similar the experiences are, despite the fact that the preceding cognitive deficits are caused by a large variety of neurological disorders (i.e., different types of dementia, strokes, brain tumors, etc.). As our own and earlier data suggest, the disorder seemed to have no impact whatsoever on any of the characteristics of the TL episode (such as cognitive function during the episode, length, or temporal proximity to death). These results appear to suggest that there may be no single cause behind the reemergence of the "old self" before death. Any physiological regeneration would have to vary significantly, given the wide variety of processes underlying these disorders. Clearly, then, additional research into the possible mechanisms that enable, trigger, or cause TL is warranted. As a first step, we hoped the triggers of lucid episodes hypothesized by the respondents would provide some clues into this question.

But only a few case descriptions carried such information, and when I specifically asked some of the respondents whether certain conditions might have triggered the lucid episode, most pointed at the lack of any special circumstances or events that may have led to the lucid episode—other than the fact that the patient was dying: "No. It came as quite a surprise, as did his death." "No. Nothing at all out of the ordinary. But she died the next day." "She was dying." "No, except we knew death was quickly approaching." "I don't remember any particular thing associated with it. Everybody was just so stunned to see it happening and enjoying the last moments with her. But the doctors had told us that she was about to die soon." "I can only think of the fact that she was dying. Otherwise, no trigger." "Well, he died. How about that for a trigger?"

Other than that, some respondents mentioned the visits of friends and family members as possible triggers: "Visits from her children. They didn't know she had terminal cancer." "Brothers came from out of town to visit my father-in-law." "Visiting relatives perhaps; everyone in her family rallied around within a day of her hospitalization." "She was in hospital at the time for end-of-life care. Relatives were visiting at the time. She had been unresponsive for the previous two days."

However, reports that link family visits to terminal lucidity should be read with some caution as they may have the sequence of events backward. It is equally possible that the presence of family members and friends does not trigger the lucid episode, but rather that family members naturally are more likely to note a marked difference in the patient. In other words, the fact that a terminal episode was observed logically presupposes the presence of visitors; it does not follow, however, that it was therefore triggered by said visitors. Moreover, since the overwhelming majority of the reported cases occurred shortly before dying, the presence of family members and friends might also simply have been due to their wanting to be present at the patient's bed when their health was known to be declining, once again reversing the putative relationship between family visits and terminal lucidity.

Few informants referred to changes in medication as a potential cause or trigger of the TL episode: in two cases, lucidity was attributed to discontinued medication such as chemotherapy: "only decision to stop chemo on Monday (two days previous)" and "dementia medications"; "The doctors took him off his dementia medications. His family thought maybe that was why he was so much better"; and two participants mentioned change of healthcare setting as potential triggers or contributing factors: "the removal from hospital into a nursing home"; "transfer from the hospital to a hospice house."

No respondent mentioned any other potential triggers (weather, time of day, special life events). The only physiological factor repeatedly mentioned was thus the impending death of the patient, beyond which there were no clear indications of external triggers.

"A Lot of Peace and Acceptance": Reactions

And then there is the question of how family members, relatives, and friends react to witnessing a TL episode. Although this is not the central topic of the book, I will briefly discuss it at this juncture, because respondents often wanted to more than just relate what they had experienced and seen; most of them also tried to understand the phenomenon, to grasp the implications, and, not least, to come to terms with the unexpected return before the final separation from their family member or friend—the improbable combination of a joyful and saddening event at the same time. After all, TL merges two events that would individually suffice to act as a psychological stressor: first, the unexpected "return" of a person who had been "lost"—sometimes for years on end. And, second, the subsequent passing of this person, whether hours, days, or at most a few weeks later.

It is sometimes said that death is "deliverance" to those who suffer from dementia. Such notions may help relatives to cope with the death of their loved one; they frame it as a positive event, both for those who are dying and those who are left behind. From my conversations and correspondence with caregivers, I learned that some are reluctant to admit even to themselves that when the patient is getting increasingly confused, restless, delusional, or aggressive, they hope that all of this will end, somehow or other. Most also say that they feel guilty for even hoping that this life will come to a natural end. But what, then, if some unknown element or factor during the dying process temporarily releases the person from her illness *before* the onset of death? This can be a deeply unsettling and confusing experience. And the experience becomes more complex when we consider that most also describe their last encounter with the relative or friend as beautiful, deeply satisfying, sacred, special, and unique. "When I think of it, I cry and smile at the same time," the witnesses tell us: "I long for reliving it, and at the same time, I am happy that it is over. What can I say? I am just grateful and confused." Indeed, a sizable number of our respondents felt overwhelmingly grateful for being granted an unexpected last opportunity to say goodbye to their beloved relative or friend:

> My mother's lucidity before dying was a wonderful gift, which made her passing so much easier to accept. I also saw her old loving self in the conversation we had. After so much emotional hardship with the dementia it was good to know she was leaving our reality as herself.

> It was wonderful to have those final moments/hours with them—to have all the pain and suffering they endured disappear if only for that brief moment in time. It helps so much with the grieving process.

> At first surprise with the enlightening feeling and opportunity to say and hear something important. Very emotional and rewarding experience.

> The last bit of communication brought all of us a lot of peace and acceptance of our life conditions. I definitely cherish those moments when I remember that I was the last person to interact with her, my name was the last word she spoke, and the way I was able to be with her throughout her illness, no regrets.

This was soooo wonderful, moving! I was so happy and grateful.

It was a gift and a blessing to me as I had things I needed to say to him.

Some, however, also mentioned being "shocked" or confused by the lucid episode:

Even though he had been unresponsive all day, I spoke to him and told him I was there. To my dismay, he woke up and started asking about family members.

For a moment I had hope that she would get better but she quickly declined and passed away just six days later.

Everyone was shocked. We thought it was the end. She just sat up and started talking to everyone like nothing was happening. She was smiling and engaging in conversation like she would normally. Everyone was so confused but happy to have that time with her. It did not last long.

I am very bewildered. I have no idea what happened. I know that I should be happy, and I am. But I am also very confused.

In further correspondence with the group of informants who had experienced the lucid episode as a mixed blessing, a psychologically interesting phenomenon emerged. Some said that they had found their own way to deal with the illness and slow deterioration, with the often bizarre behavioral and personality changes of their ill relative: they bid farewell while the person in question was still alive. This dissociation describes a coping mechanism that occasionally occurs among family members in case of severe—physical as well as mental—illness. It spares them the daily disappointment, disquiet, and pain of the personality changes of their relative or friend. It enables them to keep their relative or friend in memory in the state before dementia struck, and it makes it easier for them to differentiate between who this person was and how he or she is now. But this coping mechanism collapses the moment the patient, already bidden farewell to during her lifetime, suddenly and wholly unexpectedly "returns." And not only does it collapse; some think and fear that they had bid farewell far too early. They feel guilty.

Who helps these relatives to make sense of what they've experienced? Who reassures them that they are not alone, and that their reaction is nothing out of the ordinary, nothing to be ashamed of, but simply human? Who tells them that it is fine to accept that life can be as bewildering as death and that, if the death of a relative includes unexpected events such as terminal lucidity, it *is* indeed highly bewildering, even to the helping professionals? In brief, someone has to be there and assist those left behind in coping, understanding, and coming to terms with their experience.

Hope in Hopeless Places

And it does not stop here: for one also needs to assist those who did not witness an episode of terminal lucidity—a problem that I believe will become acute once terminal lucidity becomes better known in the public discourse. We again find parallels to the situation in the early days of near-death experience research. Early skepticism within the medical profession about whether near-death experiences were real at all was gradually replaced by the question of how to do justice, from a medical and psychological perspective, to those who report such experiences. But what about those who come near death and do not have, or do not remember having, an NDE? This is clearly an understudied subject, but one occasionally hears from this group that they feel almost betrayed because they did not have one of those wonderful experiences everybody talks about. Few listen to those who have little to report, but who nonetheless face the very same existential questions as those who did have an NDE.

It is easy to imagine how and why something similar may happen with TL, too, especially given the public TL narrative. When the first reports of our work on terminal lucidity appeared in popular media, they were largely written on a note of hope—probably because some of the journalists quickly recognized that terminal lucidity represents a very positive alternative to the usual bleak narratives of decline and destruction one normally associates with Alzheimer's, dementia, or other such severe neurological disorders. Without doubt, this is a justifiable view of the phenomenon.

But one should not forget nor hide the fact that terminal lucidity still remains a relatively rare occurrence. The only available prospective study thus far (Macleod) suggests that some 6 percent of the dying experience an episode of terminal lucidity; but the patient collective was limited (one hundred persons) and not directly comparable to our preselected group of cognitively impaired patients. The Korean study has retrospectively observed the smallest incidence so far, at a teaching hospital in Ilsan: six cases of terminal lucidity out of 338 deaths (1.8 percent)—however, only one of these patients suffered from dementia. Peter Fenwick reports a much higher number—14 percent.[7] Informal interviews I held at hospices and palliative care units also suggest a wide variety of estimates. Some medical personnel say that they "frequently" observe TL, whereas others never seem to have encountered it. So the numbers are obviously vague estimates and only additional prospective studies will help us get a clearer picture.

The difficulty in arriving at a realistic estimate of the incidence of

TL is additionally complicated by the fact that TL can pass unnoticed. Given the relatively short time window in which most terminally lucid episodes take place, it is quite possible that a number of such lucid episodes take place when nobody is present to record and report them. This point was also raised by several respondents, who mentioned that they "almost missed" the patient's return to lucidity as they originally had other plans for the day of their visit, or, in some cases, nearly did not make it to the hospital during visiting times due to traffic or other intervening circumstances.

In any case, responsible reporting on TL will, I believe, always need to include the declaration that TL appears to be a rare phenomenon. Sadly, most patients suffering from dementia or other neurological disorders die without experiencing a noticeable episode of terminal lucidity. It would therefore be irresponsible and unethical to instill in family members undue hope that their ill relatives will have a lucid episode. I regularly receive emails from relatives and friends who hoped or hope for TL—sometimes even expect it, only to be gravely disappointed when the patient dies without a return to lucidity:

> When my father's health declined, I made sure to be with him as much as possible, desperately hoping for a last chance to say good-bye. I so, so, so hoped for a last hooray, but sadly, it never came. When I read all these wonderful stories on "terminal lucidity," I am both moved and sad. It would have been so important to me. It makes me very sad.

> Read about your work last year. Now Mum has dementia and now has pneumonia. Writing this from my iPhone. I am with her every moment so I will not miss her terminal lucidity. Any chance to help her getting through? I talk to her and hope she will hear. So far, no trace of lucidity.

We were waiting anxiously for his return. There was so much I wanted to tell Dad. Assure him that we will take care of Mum. That I made peace with my brother. That all was fine and that he need not worry. I was with him every hour. But he died without any sign of it. He was gone. I would like to know why. I often wonder why. We so much needed this closure.

And here arises a moral dilemma for researchers working on TL: on the one hand, TL offers the possibility to study a remarkable phenomenon with potentially wide-ranging implications on so many layers—medical, psychological, philosophical, even spiritual. So as a researcher, you want to talk about it. You want people to know that occasionally, something very remarkable—and remarkably beautiful at that—can happen near death. And you want people, especially members of the helping professions, to know so that they know how to react when they witness it; or when they ought to assist bewildered family members of patients to make the most of the gift they have been granted. And yet, as long as we know so little about the phenomenon itself and its triggers or precursors, caution must be applied in informing relatives and friends of patients suffering cognitive impairment about the possibility of terminal lucidity, without at the same time raising unrealistic hopes or expectations that are likely to remain unfulfilled.

At the same time, relatives and visitors should be informed about the possibility that, if such episodes occur, they tend to be relatively short and *might* perhaps be related to the impending death of the patient. It is a fine balance between making people aware of terminal lucidity so that they don't miss what many describe as a beautiful experience—a last gift—and instilling unrealistic hopes in those who will perhaps never receive this gift. As with so many things related to death and dying, terminal lucidity is—at least for the moment—not predictable, nor can you plan around it. We can only be ready, without demanding or expecting it.

In summary: terminal lucidity is not limited to different types of dementia, but more generally seems to be a phenomenon spanning a variety of neurological disorders. Episodes of lucidity seem to substantially exceed normal daily variations in the cognitive and mental state of a person suffering from a neurologically and cognitively impairing disorder, and occur in the course of illnesses that generally preclude remission. Finally, available data strongly suggest that terminal lucidity is a death-related phenomenon, though there is some uncertainty due to possible response bias. And ambiguity remains with regard to the actual incidence of the phenomenon.

But it does occur, and in the next chapters, we will explore what it tells us about us, its meaning, and about death and dying.

PART III

Mind at Death, Mind at Large

That our being should consist of two fundamental elements
[physical and psychical] offers I suppose no greater inherent
improbability than that it should rest on one only.

—Sir Charles S. Sherrington

9

White Crows

What Is TL Trying to Tell Us?

When I try to explain to others what our studies on terminal lucidity are all about, I often say something along the lines of: "We study whether, and if so, when, why, and how people with dementia seem to 'wake up' to their former, pre-morbid selves when close to death. It doesn't happen too often, but often enough to warrant further study. It's all very galvanizing and not nearly as depressing as you might think given that we study dementia and death."

And when people inquire further, I usually add: "There's much consolation to be found in this field, unlikely as it may sound. And there are myriads of implications. Most of them are somehow deeply reassuring, and we try to understand what our findings tell us about ourselves, and about the relationship between our personhood and what goes on in our brains." It is an easy and accessible brief description of our work, and it explains why I have been working in this field for so many years, and why I plan on staying within this field. And it does, I believe, cover most of what we are currently doing—collecting cases and circumstances of terminal lucidity, and pondering what terminal lucidity is all about: listening to and learning valuable lessons from our study participants and those who are dying.

In the beginning, I didn't expect that people would further inquire about this line of research after listening to my brief description. After all, despite my reassurance that our work is not nearly as depressing as people may think, neither dementia nor death are particularly uplifting or entertaining conversation topics at, let's say, a dinner or garden party. But many—many more, in fact, than I ever would have expected—inquire further, and I am often amazed by how quickly they catch some of the more subtle aspects of my brief description. "What do you mean by *seeming* to wake up'?" someone may ask. "How can you *seem* to wake up? If you wake up, you wake up—that's not something you can simulate, no? If you successfully imitate that you woke up, you obviously woke up in the first place." And even more frequently they ask: "So if their old self wakes up, as you say, doesn't that mean it must have been there then all along, but perhaps overshadowed by their illness?" And then, the discussions begin. Occasionally someone reports that he or she witnessed TL in a relative or friend, others join in, and before you know it, you find yourself in the midst of a deeply philosophical or religious debate about the brain and mind, about the soul, about a possible future of the soul after TL and death, and so on. Clearly, there is an intuitive pull in TL—perhaps not least because it tells such a very different story about dementia, decline, and death than we are mostly accustomed to hear.

Contrast this with the story of Mrs. D as told by Paul Edwards (see page 34), and the ostensibly "inescapable" bleak message about dementia and other neurological diseases he derived from it: that our mind is nothing but what is happening in our brains, and that therefore, disease and disorder, and finally the disintegration of neuronal functions, entails the erosion, and the complete dissolution of ourselves, our minds, our personhood, and our memories.

As we saw, at least at first, Paul Edwards's message appeared to be quite persuasive. However, I also asked whether the argument would still be as persuasive if Mrs. D had "woken up again" at her deathbed—and without us having the slightest reason to believe that the condition of her brain, so mercilessly attacked by the progression of her Alzheimer's, had suddenly disappeared overnight. As the previous chapter shows, this is no longer a merely hypothetical question; rather, it is a phenomenon that has been, and continues to be, witnessed and documented hundreds of times over.

What follows from this? How are we to interpret terminal lucidity? A simple—but too simple—answer would be to take Edwards's argument that one can draw strong conclusions about the nature and destiny of the self from what one observes in dementia, and apply it to what we now know about terminal lucidity. According to Edwards (and to materialism in general), the decline and destruction of the self along with the progression of dementia is taken to be strong evidence against a self beyond brain function—evidence against the soul, if you will. Then what is the spontaneous and unexpected return of that very same old self despite dementia or other underlying neurological disease evidence of? Does the fact that a spontaneous reemergence of the intact person suggest—in line with Eccles's and Frankl's theory of a personal and conscious selfhood beyond neurobiology—that this "old self" had *not* been completely destroyed by the neurological disease process in the first place? That it has somehow been preserved and sheltered, though rendered inaccessible as a result of the disease process?

So clearly, TL raises a number of questions—and in fact, more than it answers. For instance, one question we repeatedly discussed in our research meetings is: If terminal lucidity is possible at all, why does it occur at the point of death and not before, when it would argu-ably be much more useful and, evolutionarily speaking, much more adaptive? Why does it not happen earlier, when we would have much more to gain from the spontaneous remission of dementia? And given that TL seems to be primarily death-related, what exactly happens with the person at and around death that enables such an unexpected and in fact highly improbable event to occur?

There are two lines of thought that follow from these questions. The first is clinical—if a return of lucidity can happen, perhaps it is possible to simulate or stimulate an as of yet unknown process that happens near the end of life and somehow "trigger" TL, but with-out actually endangering the life of the patient. If we found such a biomarker of TL, we could try to evoke the events that lead to TL in a controlled manner, thereby facilitating paradoxical, rather than terminal, lucidity. Perhaps, then, in the very long run, TL may lead to new therapeutic approaches for dementia and other severe neurolog-ical disorders. Tens of millions would be positively affected by this—millions, that is, who are either already ill, or know that they have a high genetic risk of developing one of the dementias. In our white paper on TL—one of the outcomes of our expert workshop at the National Institute on Aging at the NIH in Bethesda—we raised this possibility, and it is one reason why the NIA subsequently sent out a very generous funding opportunity of several million US dollars for terminal or paradoxical lucidity research.[1]

But during our discussions at the NIA expert workshop in Bethesda, we also addressed the question of the philosophical implica-tions of TL, among them the very question my conversation partners posed and pose when I briefly describe the main gist of our research work on TL: "Does it mean that the self is somehow preserved even when it seems to be severely compromised, or even 'destroyed,' just until TL actually occurs?"

Squaring a Circle

Perhaps it does; but once again, it is not that simple. For whatever we believe or speculate about the deeper meaning of TL, we will need to reconcile two very contradictory observations. On the one hand, both everyday life and a large body of research tells us that there is a pronounced dependence of our conscious mind on brain function. When we get drunk, or we have a fever, or are otherwise physiologically depleted, our minds are clouded, our sense of self may change or decline—or we may even fall unconscious altogether. Clearly, none of the many findings that attest to the dependence of mind on bodily, especially neurological, function and intactness lose any of their validity just because we encounter one single phenomenon which might appear to suggest otherwise. This dependency is, after all, what makes the dementias and other brain disorders so devastating—and, at the same time, what makes TL so remarkable. Ignoring or discarding this dependency just because TL seems to suggest otherwise, albeit in near-death circumstances, would do injustice both to the dementias and to TL.

We therefore face the challenge of reconciling two very different, conflicting observations on the relationship between self and personhood and brain function, and to find an overarching model that can accommodate both: dependency during most of our everyday lives, apparent breaches of this dependency near death.

But where to even start? There is not much scientific or theoretical work that our research group could draw on for this undertaking. There have been few attempts to further study and comprehend TL, let alone its implications, as such. Nor do we find many such attempts in earlier writings when TL was given more attention. The Victorian doctors, for example, looked at it primarily from a diagnostic angle, noting that TL usually was a sure sign that the patient would soon decline and die:

> Instances occur, not very rarely, where the delirium ceases and the mind again for a time becomes clear and sensations keen, to be followed, however, by a return of delirium, or it may be of coma, or a rapid sinking of all the bodily powers and speedily death. But along with the temporary clearing of the mental powers, and in proof of its illusiveness, there are the usual signs of bodily failure—a pinching of the features, coldness of the surface, cold sweats, and a feeble rapid pulse.[2]

Few—such as Happich and Wittneben, who witnessed and wrote about the earlier mentioned case of Käthe (see page 49), went a step further. They quoted her case in their pleas against the then burgeoning "euthanasia movement" in Germany during the early 1930s:

> For me, the most mentally deranged idiot is not inferior to normal persons in the deepest sense. I have lived through various virtually shattering experiences, some of which I have experienced together with the chief physician of our institution, Dr. Wittneben. These experiences have shown me that even the most miserable imbecile leads a hidden inner life which is just as valuable as my own inner life. It is only the destructed surface that hinders him to show it to the outside. Often in the last hours before death, all pathological obstructions fell away and revealed an inner life of such beauty, that we could only stand in front of it, feeling shaken to the core. For somebody who has witnessed such events, the entire question of legally controlled euthanasia is completely finished.[3]

And yet until very recently, there have been no concerted efforts to further study, let alone understand and explain TL. TL is a rare event, and confronts us with an unlikely incident that, as just discussed, contradicts much, if not most, accepted knowledge about the brain-mind relationship. It is, for lack of a better word, an exceptional and deeply counterintuitive phenomenon, and understanding, let alone explaining, exceptional and deeply counterintuitive phenomena is not an easy undertaking. More than that, it also challenges researchers who work in this field to move beyond what—given the phenomenon in question—may turn out to be false certainties about what they "know," and in fact only "suspect" or "believe": "Mind is what the brain does. And if the brain does nothing, there is no mind, no consciousness, no self. End of the story." This is what we learned at university. And this is what TL seems to bring into question.

When I discussed some of these issues with a colleague, he dryly quipped: "So you are chasing white crows. Good luck with that!" "White crows"—the term comes from one of psychology's most accomplished pioneers, William James, brother of the American novelist Henry James. During his long and successful career, William James not only founded the first psychology department at Harvard University, conducted groundbreaking research on perception in his lab, and wrote the first American textbooks on psychology (a lengthy two-volume tome of nearly fourteen hundred pages—usually known within the field as "the James," and an abridged, much smaller version, called "the Jimmy").

What is less known is that next to all of this, James also investigated "psychic" phenomena such as telepathy, clairvoyance, deathbed visions, and the like—somewhat unlikely subject matters for the founder of a fledgling academic discipline. But the often harsh criticism James received from colleagues didn't deter him from his relentless search. And after a few years into this search, it was no longer his sheer curiosity that kept him hooked. It was the fact that he personally believed to have witnessed far too many such unusual phenomena to yield to the pleas of his colleagues to turn to more serious and reliable studies.

In his 1896 Society for Psychical Research President's Address, William James discussed his position on said phenomena. He, not unlike those who study TL, found himself caught between having occasionally witnessed something quite out of the ordinary of his own scientific training, which gave him ample reason to doubt what he had witnessed. But James did not stop there, leaving these contradictions between "orthodox belief" (as he called it) and his own experiences unresolved, side by side. Rather, he describes in his presidential address that—faced with the choice of which to believe more, the scientific status quo of his time or his own experiments and observations—he came to the conclusion that the latter carried far too much weight. And not only did it, in James's opinion, carry too much weight for himself, but in fact for everyone who seriously and openly engages in dealing with the available evidence, wherever it leads to—even, or especially, when it contradicts (or appears to contradict) the status quo:

> But it is a miserable thing for a question of truth to be confined to mere presumption and counter-presumption, with no decisive thunderbolt of fact to clear the baffling darkness. And sooth to say, in talking so much of the merely presumption-weakening value of our records, I have been willfully taking the point of view of the so-called "rigorous scientific" disbeliever, and making an ad hominem plea. My own point of view is different. For me the thunderbolt has fallen, and the orthodox belief has not merely had its presumption weakened, but the truth itself of the belief is decisively overthrown. If you will let me use the language of the

professional logic-shop, a universal proposition can be made untrue by a particular instance.

If you wish to upset the law that all crows are black, you mustn't seek to show that all crows are black; it is enough if you prove one single crow to be white.[4]

Whether or not James's assessment of the strength of the evidence for psychic phenomena is accurate, my colleague's remarks were apt; we were chasing white crows. At least at first sight, a universal proposition (mind-brain dependence) appears to need revision because of a particular instance: TL would then be another white crow. If—and that is a very strong "if"—that is what TL is really telling us.

One of the foremost questions about TL is whether it, too, is a white crow phenomenon at all. Are there other white crow cases in which a relative independence of self, mind, and personhood from severely disordered brain activity can be observed? If so, do these additional phenomena support our TL observations and thus tip the balance toward a non-materialist essence of personhood? As the American psychologist Paul Francis Cunningham points out:

All one needs is a single solid finding where normal cognitive processes happen in the absence of requisite brain material, or when awareness occurs in the absence of measurable brain functioning, to change the way one thinks about the relationship between mind and body.[5]

An ideal place to look for similar cases is, as Cunningham suggests, when severe hypo-function, perhaps even extinction of brain function, is approaching, while verifiable mental activity still continues to unfold. Or if such activity is, as we observe in TL, restored and enhanced when a person comes closer to death.

10

Mind and Brain in Extreme States

Mind and Brain near Death

But where do we find such a state of absent or at least strongly compromised brain function, if not when people are either severely impaired due to brain disease or, alternatively, when they are very close to death? There is one striking aspect of TL that may hold a key in this regard—it is the fact that TL occurs in an enormously wide variety of underlying neurological disorders (dementia without specifier, Alzheimer's, Lewy body dementia, cardiovascular dementia, AIDS-related dementia, brain abscesses, stroke, primary or secondary brain tumors, late effects of bacterial meningitis, traumatic brain injury, etc.). Next to its defining feature—the spontaneous and unexpected return of mental lucidity, i.e., the "old self"—the common denominator of TL episodes is the fact that they take place close to the patient's death. Otherwise, the physiological underpinnings of one case seem to have very little in common with the other. As we saw in the previous chapter, in our search for possible correlates or individual factors or situational circumstances and triggers, we found absolutely nothing that would enable us to predict or expect TL in a specific group of patients: diagnosis played no role, age played no role, neither did gender. The only possible factor repeatedly mentioned by our study participants was that the patients were (a) severely cognitively impaired, and (b) that most of them were about to die within a relatively short time window.

So, given the significant concentration of such cases near death, one naturally takes notice—and does so all the more because TL is not the only unusual psychological phenomenon that occurs in the vicinity of death. In our white paper on TL, we briefly discussed the parallels of TL and the near-death experience (NDE), that is, the complex and phenomenologically and spiritually rich conscious experience that some patients report after having been resuscitated (more on this in a moment). During our research workshop at the NIA, we had lengthy discussions on the parallels between TL and the NDE. These parallels are in fact both striking and profound: for just as in TL, in the NDE, too, we find complex thought and conscious experience, self-consciousness and personhood when they are—given impaired brain states during, for example, cardiac arrest—highly unlikely.

And here again, the common factor between any NDEs is that they take place near death. Otherwise, there is no certain known factor or variable that would enable us to predict who will remember and report an NDE after having survived cardiac and/or respiratory arrest:

> NDEs have been reported across cultures since antiquity and are arguably the phenomena most closely aligned with paradoxical lucidity in dementia, especially when the latter occurs just before death. NDEs represent phenomenologically rich experiences in the setting of a hypofunctioning brain. Similar to paradoxical lucidity in dementia, NDEs were primarily reported anecdotally, retrospectively, or in case studies until the early 2000s. In 2001, two prospective

epidemiological studies in cohorts of patients who had cardiac arrest revealed that the incidence of NDEs in this population could be as high as 18 percent, which is substantially more common than that which might have been predicted from case reports alone.[1]

So why is it that precisely at the decisive crossroads of death and dying, when the biological machinery of our brains ceases to function appropriately, we find that an active mental life is even possible? And that we thus observe a phenomenon that seems to run so clearly counter to the observations made under more ordinary circumstances—dependence of the mind on intact and structured brain function? Another white crow? And why do both appear only near death?

To understand what might be going on here, it is helpful to make a brief excursion into the history of science and scientific development. It is easily accessible, and deals with the question of what we do with and where we usually find white crows in general—and how this may inform us about how we deal with TL and NDE.

At the Limits: Boundary Conditions

When we try to understand something—scientifically or in everyday life—we usually first observe things and events, note their regularities, and then develop theories about what these things and events are and how they behave, on the basis of which we hope to predict their future behavior. This may strike the reader as a somewhat convoluted way to explain how understanding comes about—but think of it from an everyday life perspective, and it all becomes much clearer. If you begin to understand something better—be it your smartphone, an app, or even your car—it means that it no longer surprises you with as much unforeseen behavior as it did before you came to understand it better. You begin to know it; and that means that you start knowing how to handle it: when I press this button, that happens; when I start this function, that happens. First, there'll be many surprises; but as your familiarity with the device grows, there'll be fewer and fewer. Your predictions become increasingly accurate. The scientific process usually is a bit more controlled and ordered than playing around with and finding out how our smartphones work, but the general procedure is all the same: you become increasingly familiar with a thing or a phenomenon, and you discover that things don't just "somehow" happen, but that there are regular sequences of events. There appears to be a certain "logic" behind it all (there is, and you are about to find out). Then we build a theory around what we understand about the regularities. And if we begin to understand something a little better—if a theory turns out well—it will align with our background knowledge, it will not inflate entities and functions beyond what is absolutely necessary, and, most important, it will accurately predict the behavior of things and events. Then, the theory passed the test, at least for the moment.

But simply knowing—or having a good theory—is not actually what science (or, in everyday life, understanding) is all about. It's also about discovery, about being curious, about reaching out, about provoking nature, testing its limits, if you will, to reveal more of its inner workings. So, when we understand something, we also like to see and test how far our understanding goes, and perhaps also, where its limits may lie. So we look at more exotic cases—we test how our understanding fares in more unusual or extreme conditions. For example: Do heavy things fall faster than lighter objects? Of course they do; we can observe this every day—a book hits the ground sooner than a feather or a single piece of paper. But is this also true in a vacuum? No. Surprisingly, it isn't; in a vacuum both fall down with the same speed, and this must be accounted for. Or do very, very small objects follow the same mechanics as very, very large objects? No, they don't, and so this, too, must be accounted for. Often, such observations at the more extreme end turned out to be signposts for a better, deeper, and more complete understanding of the larger spectrum of what is being studied. For as we get deeper into exotic or extreme conditions of certain natural phenomena, certain laws and regularities supposedly carved in stone might precipitously lose their validity, as nature reveals hitherto hidden properties and aspects not seen under everyday conditions. White crows abound. Often, fundamentally different models are needed to account for these white crows and, accordingly, new models and theories have to be developed.

Greyson's Proposal

Why is this relevant for our attempts to understand TL? My colleague Bruce Greyson—with whom I published the first large-scale study on contemporary TL cases in dementia—was, as far I know, the first to propose that what holds for the role of boundary conditions for physics might also help us understand the role of death and dying in TL and the NDE. The reasoning is fairly straightforward: death undoubtedly is an extreme condition of and for the organism (and the person), and thus represents yet another case in which extreme conditions reveal new insights about nature—in this case: about our nature. If we therefore apply the general notion of "domain-specific" behavior to things and processes, it might be less surprising why the states near death repeatedly confront us with findings that contradict what we regularly and reliably observe in everyday life, the lab, and in clinical work. In a lecture given at the United Nations in New York, Bruce Greyson elaborated on these parallels as follows:

Newtonian mechanics was accepted for several hundred years as a description of this wonderful clockwork world we live in. Newtonian mechanics works very well for most of our daily lives: when you throw something up it falls down, all the time. The harder you throw it, the faster it goes. It is only when you get to the extremes, measuring extremely small particles or extremely fast speeds, that the Newtonian model breaks down. It is not that Newton was wrong, it is just that the formulas he was using describe a limited case. And when we get to the extreme examples, his formulas no longer work and we need relativity to make corrections. [...]

I think the same thing is going on with the brain and the mind. In our everyday life, assuming that the brain and the mind are the same thing works relatively fine. It is only when you get to the extreme cases such as when the brain stops functioning that you see the formula breaking down, that the brain and the mind do not seem to be the same thing.

The most common example is the near-death experience, when you have many people who appear to be dead, and a few people who actually have a flat EEG line being documented, who come back, saying: "Not only was I thinking, but I was thinking more clearly than I ever have before." We also have other examples of cases when the brain is compromised, people think more clearly. There are exceptional cases of people who have irreversible dementia, or severe mental illness, who in the dying moments, before they die, become perfectly lucid. They start recognizing family members, they start talking coherently, they lose their delusions, and then they die. What is that all about? We do not have a materialistic explanation for this. If you assume that

mind and brain can separate when the brain starts deterio-
rating, then you have an explanation.[2]

At this point, however, the idea that the dependence of our personality and selfhood on brain function may be domain-specific—the
domain being everyday life—is merely a vaguely plausible suggestion;
an attempt to make the implausible (TL) a little bit more plausible.
But there are ways to go further than that. Ways to find out whether
there might be more to it than mere plausibility. For should there indeed be more to Greyson's suggestion, we should expect there to be
more such improbable consciousness phenomena near death. In other
words—perhaps we find more white crows in the gray area between
life and death.

11

Mind at Death

Mindsight

One such case, as already pointed out, is the NDE, especially those selected cases that occur during clinical death and/or are taking place when the EEG cannot detect any brain activity, but nevertheless, to all appearances, people have complex and orderly conscious (and often strikingly beautiful) experiences.

A second category, again related to death, I will mention only briefly because it is so extremely rare, and it's therefore still uncertain what it means. But if verified, it would be a rather impressive white crow. Ever since near-death experiences have been studied more systematically (beginning in the late 1970s), there have been reports scattered in the literature of blind patients claiming to have had visual experiences during their NDE. Together with Sharon Cooper, my friend and colleague American psychologist and NDE pioneer Kenneth Ring has located a total of twenty-one such cases of legally blind persons who reported that they could "see" during their NDE (but

not before, and not after their NDE). He baptized this phenomenon
with the apt name "mindsight." Some of the witnesses interviewed for
Ken's and Sharon Cooper's articles and book on mindsight were blind
from birth; others had lost their sight after the age of five; the rest were
legally blind but had weak residual visual abilities (i.e., although these
patients cannot see colors, shapes, or people, they can still tell the difference between light and dark—but nothing beyond that):

> One of our interviewees whose sight perished completely
> as a result of a stroke at age twenty-two, and was near-
> sighted before that, told us in connection with seeing her
> body, her doctor, and the operating room during her NDE:
> "I know I could see and I was supposed to be blind. . . .
> And I know I could see everything. . . . It was very clear
> when I was out. I could see details and everything."
>
> Another man, who had lost his vision in a car accident at
> the age of nineteen, had a comforting vision of his deceased
> grandmother across a valley during his NDE. In comment-
> ing on his clarity, he said: "Of course I had no sight because
> I had total destruction of my eyes in the accident, but [my
> vision] was very clear and distinct. . . . I had perfect vision in
> that experience."
>
> Still another man, this one blind from birth, found himself
> in an enormous library during the transcendental phase of his
> NDE and saw "thousands and millions and billions of books,
> as far as you could see." Asked if he saw them visually he said,
> "Oh, yes!" Did he see them clearly? "No problem." Was he
> surprised at being able to see thus? "Not in the least. I said,
> 'Hey, you can't see,' and I said, 'Well, of course I can see. Look
> at those books. That's ample proof that I can see.'" Typically,
> vision is reported as clear, even acutely so, by our respondents
> [. . .]; seeing is often described as "perfectly natural" or "the

way it's supposed to be." However, sometimes the initial onset of visual perception of the physical world is disorienting
and even disturbing to the blind.[1]

As might be expected, these very unusual claims have been met
with ample skepticism. Critics have suggested that these reports may
be simple confabulations (if not outright inventions), or that they are
in fact based on false memories, constructed on the basis of other sen-
sory perceptions (e.g. auditory or tactile), that no visual perception actually took place and the respondents mistakenly reconstructed and
recounted auditory or other sensations in visual terms. Given what we
know about how constructive memory works, this may well be what
happened in some cases.[2]

However, it must also be pointed out that the fact that critics read-
ily assume the usually quite vivid descriptions of the respondents to
be either fabrications or false memories begs the question: if one is
not prepared to even consider events or data that seem to contradict
"common knowledge" (white crows) precisely *because* they contradict
"common knowledge," it is only a small step from open-ended scientific inquiry to dogmatism, i.e., the very opposite of the curiosity-
driven discovery process described above. If every white crow you see
is written off as being an illusion, a false memory, an error, or an in-
tentional lie, if the white crow might sit right before you, stare you in
the face, and yet you decide to deny its presence, then you are ignoring
writing on the wall. Witnessing an event warrants further investigation, and, should it turn out to be real and reliable, perhaps a revision
of what we up to that point believed to know.

Nevertheless, the fact that unexpected findings sometimes pave the
way to a more comprehensive understanding of nature does not mean
that we have to take *every* unexpected observation at face value, and
then prematurely overthrow well-established theories or models. Only
if we find more such cases, and are able to validate them, would the

evidence from mindsight be less easy to ignore. But strong evidence must be reliable evidence, and so far, no mindsight cases reported in the literature are sufficiently corroborated (or supported by other evidence). I mention these reports on mindsight in order to illustrate the findings we would have to establish in order to gain more insight into TL.

NDEs

The situation is very different today with the NDE, though it, too, was first met with similar skepticism, if not outright rejection and suspicion. Early pioneers in NDE studies thus often had to convince their colleagues that the NDEs actually represented a real phenomenon and legitimate object of research in the first place—meaning that a critical number of persons had rich, complex, and structured experiences while lying seemingly unconscious in the ER, for the most part suffering from cardiac or respiratory arrest or both, i.e., clinical death. But for (far) too long, it was insinuated that near-death experiencers had been taken in by illusory memories, or psychodynamic defense mechanisms, or other malfunctions and tricks of their own minds.[3]

At times they also faced accusations of having freely invented their NDEs from beginning to end—just as researchers working in this area were accused of operating outside the scientific discourse, or of being more concerned with religion and spirituality than with serious scientific research. The situation has since changed, however, not least due to the sheer power of numbers: according to several international studies, NDEs occur in up to 18 percent of the cohort of patients who come close to death, which makes for a large figure of several million NDErs worldwide, and accordingly, a large number of medical personnel and researchers being confronted with such reports. Too many, it seems, to be ignored or written off as mere confabulations or fabrications.

A thought experiment suggested by NDE researcher Mally Cox-Chapman might be useful here: If a patient told you that while clinically dead, she had a near-death experience, experienced a detailed life review, had the impression of "leaving the body," remembered seeing beautiful "otherworldly" landscapes or colors or lights never seen before, etc., you would, in all likelihood, listen politely, perhaps wondering whether this patient should see a mental health professional or perhaps a priest or rabbi. If ten, or a hundred patients confided in you that they had a near-death experience while clinically dead, you'd probably listen more closely. But what if millions of patient told the same story?[4] There comes a point where ignoring such accounts is simply no longer possible; and given that never have so many people been successfully resuscitated since the mid-to late 1970s, it was to be expected that the NDE was finally accepted as a real phenomenon and research on NDEs would become a burgeoning research field, with papers appearing in numerous journals of medicine, psychiatry, psychology, sociology, theology, philosophy, and other disciplines. It is no exaggeration to say that today, the subject of near-death studies—for long a niche and fringe topic within academia—has become a central topic of research in the psychology of death and dying.

12

Perception at the End of Life

When Do NDEs Take Place?

At the same time, not every NDE occurs in actual objective, physiological proximity to death. Not all NDEs are therefore equally suitable to test Greyson's proposal of a domain-specific relationship of brain and personhood. NDEs or rather NDE-like experiences are occasionally also reported by those who *subjectively* believed themselves to be close to death while in fact their medical condition was not even close to being life-threatening at all. Yet *thinking* that you are about to die is quite different from actual *physiological* closeness to death, or even clinical death itself.

The following discussion will therefore be limited to NDEs that occurred during cardiac and/or respiratory arrest. And even within this group, we have to meet a few conditions in order to test Greyson's proposal: we first need to ascertain that the NDEs took place *during* the cardiac and/or respiratory arrest, and not thereafter when physiological function and sufficient oxygen saturation returns. For only then do we encounter a phenomenon that shares with TL the main—and puzzling—feature of lucid and complex conscious experience during a time of brain dysfunction: in the case of TL due to the underlying brain disease leading to dementia, and in the case of the NDE due to the fact that, for example, in full cardiac arrest, brain function basically shuts down altogether within only a few seconds:

> Whether the heart actually stops beating entirely or goes into ventricular fibrillation, the result is essentially instantaneous circulatory arrest, with blood flow and oxygen uptake in the brain plunging swiftly to near-zero levels. EEG signs of cerebral ischemia, typically with global slowing and loss of fast activity, are detectable within six to ten seconds and progress to isoelectricity (flat-line EEGs) within ten to twenty seconds of the onset of arrest. In sum, full arrest leads rapidly to the three major clinical signs of death (absence of cardiac output, absence of respiration, and absence of brainstem reflexes) and provides the best model we have of the dying process.[1]

So clearly, NDE during cardiac or respiratory arrest could be helpful for understanding TL. In both cases, death and dying are linked to heightened, rather than diminished, mental alertness with compromised brain activity. However, there's a problem: we usually do not and cannot know when exactly an NDE takes place. Rather, what typically happens is this: a resuscitated patient talks about his or her NDE (usually hours or, more typically, days after he or she has been successfully resuscitated). The NDEr will not, however, generally be able to tell us *when exactly* the NDE had taken place. He or she may tell us about a deeply moving experience, perhaps also about

an overwhelmingly beautiful otherworldly journey; but questions of
date and clock hour will probably be the least important aspect to the
NDEr, nor will he or she likely be able to tell us much about it, even
if he or she wanted to.

From the perspective of the experiencer, this is all too understandable: when you believe you have had a brief glimpse of an extraordinarily beautiful and otherworldly place, in all likelihood you wouldn't
be interested in what time it was. But as a researcher in this field, you
want to acknowledge the inner aspects and the stories people tell you,
and at the same time, you also want to generate data that go beyond
mere stories.

Thus from the researcher's point of view, the fact that we do not
know when exactly an NDE takes place poses a major problem: How
do we know that the NDE did not take place during the recovery
phase, at a time when general physiological, and especially brain function, was presumably less compromised? Before we consider the NDE
as another white crow, we therefore first need to know it actually takes
place. Given the subjective nature of the NDE—it is a deeply private,
if you will, inner, experience—researchers interested in this question
consequently tried out ways to somehow relate it to "objective" events
(and their timing). In the NDE literature, such attempts have mostly
focused on one of the very few aspects that can in principle be externally verified (and timed): the claim of a sizable percentage of NDErs
to have been "outside their bodies," and to have made visual perceptions of their immediate surroundings during that state:

> [. . .] Forty-eight percent of near-death experiencers re-
> ported seeing their physical bodies from a different visual
> perspective. Many of them also reported witnessing events
> going on in the vicinity of their body, such as the attempts
> of medical personnel to resuscitate them at the scene of an
> accident or in an emergency room.[2]

Surely, this in itself is an astonishing claim—but let's for the moment leave aside whether or not NDErs "leave their bodies" during an NDE. For our purposes, it would suffice if they have consciously accessible recollections of events that happened during their NDE, which in turn are assignable to a certain point in time of their crisis, thereby allowing us to infer when approximately the actual NDE took place.

Are Perceptions near Death Accurate?

Only a few studies have been conducted to date on external corroboration of visual perceptions during the "out-of-body" period of NDEs. The American cardiologist Michael Sabom, for example, asked a group of NDErs who suffered a cardiac arrest and had undergone cardiopulmonary resuscitation (CPR), and a patient control group who did not report an NDE, to describe the CPR procedure as if they were witnessing it from the outside. The vast majority of patients—no less than 87 percent—in the non-NDE control group made at least one major error in their descriptions of the CPR. The NDE group made none (0 percent):

> Could these accurate autoscopic reports of CPR be "false memory" accounts based on the "best guess" efforts of previously hospitalized patients? To check for this, twenty-five seasoned coronary care unit patients, with backgrounds similar to the NDE group but who had not encountered an NDE, were asked to describe CPR from the standpoint of an onlooker in the corner of a hospital room. Confidence in these descriptions appeared to be low. Two of the patients described nothing. Without undue prompting, twenty of the remaining twenty-three patients made major errors in describing salient

objects and events: "mouth to mouth breathing" for artificial respiration; "wooden throat paddles, like an ice cream stick, only bigger" for an oral airway; "a blow to the back to get the heart beating again"; "opening up the chest to place the hands around the heart and massage it"; "electric shock would be given through those wires that are fastened onto the chest and hooked up to the cardiac monitor"; "the electric shock would be given through a needle stuck in the heart through the chest"; the defibrillator paddles "would be hooked up to an air tank and pressurized" or "they would have a suction cup on the bottom of them." It would seem, therefore, that the accuracy of NDE testimonies more closely resembles true eyewitness reports than accounts that would be expected from patients who had not directly witnessed the event.[3]

In addition, some of the NDErs provided correct and detailed information about unexpected or atypical events that had taken place during their resuscitation:

Six persons claimed to have "seen" specific resuscitative details during their OBEs, including (1) the placement of an oxygen mask ("They had oxygen on me before, one of those little nose tubes, and they took that off and put on a face mask that covers your mouth and nose."); (2) a chest thump followed by external cardiac massage and insertion of airway ("He hit me right in the center of my chest. And then they were pushing on my chest . . . kinda like artificial respiration. They shoved a plastic tube, like you put in an oil can, they shoved that in my mouth."); (3) defibrillator paddles ("Well, they weren't paddles . . . they were round discs with handles on them."); (4) lubrication of the paddles ("They put something on those pads like a lubricant."); (5) positioning of the paddles ("They put one up here . . . and they put one down here."); (6) charging the defibrillator ("I think they moved the fixed needle and it stayed still while the other one moved up."); (7) defibrillation ("I thought they had given my body too much voltage. Man, my body jumped about two feet off the table."); (8) injection of intra-cardiac medications ("They put a needle in me and . . . shoved it into my chest like that."); (9) checking for pupillary response and carotid pulse ("They were pulling my eyelids up to look to see where my eyes were, I guess. . . . Then they were feeling around my neck where the pulse is."); (10) insertion of a subclavian vein catheter ("Dr. B came up and decided to put one in my left— well, not in my armpit, but on my side."); and (11) drawing arterial blood gases from the femoral artery ("shots first in the groin down there somewhere") and radial artery ("the little needle they were putting in my hand. Something about the blood gases."). When compared to medical records and cardiopulmonary resuscitation (CPR) protocol, these reports turned out to be surprisingly accurate. It is unlikely that visual details of the objects and events reported in these NDEs would have been either discussed by others present during the resuscitation or observed by the deeply arrested patient.[4]

In addition, one patient reported that he "saw" the unexpected arrival of three family members at a distant hospital location during his cardiac arrest. The accuracy of this man's report was later confirmed in separate interviews with family members.[5]

British thanatologist Penny Sartori replicated this finding in a five-year study of resuscitated cardiac arrest patients; she too found that NDErs accurately described their resuscitation, which again the control group was unable to do,[6] again suggesting not only that the NDE actually took place *during,* rather than some time *after* the resuscitation, but also that subjects were somehow able to "see" or otherwise perceive what happened in their surroundings during their NDE. And next to these few studies, there exists a large number of individual case reports of veridical perceptions during an NDE, regularly reported both in the NDE literature and at NDE congresses. These stories, too, seem to support the notion that at least some NDErs have at one time visual or other perceptions *while,* rather than *after* they were clinically dead:

> The patient, Al Sullivan, reported that, during a 1998 quadruple bypass operation, he seemed to be out of his body and watching the surgery in progress. One of the surgeons seemed to be "flapping his arms as if trying to fly." Both the surgeon and the cardiologist in this case confirmed to B. G. that the surgeon had been making these unusual movements during the surgery. The surgeon explained that, to keep his hands from touching the surface between the time he "scrubs in" and the time he actually begins the surgery, he has developed the habit of holding his hands against his chest and pointing with his elbows to give instructions to other persons in the operating room. The cardiologist confirmed that Mr. Sullivan had described this unusual behavior to him shortly after regaining consciousness following the surgery.[7]

American researcher Janice Holden further examined ninety-three similar reports of potentially verifiable perceptions during an NDE. About 43 percent of these reports could be confirmed by an independent witness, another 43 percent had an independent witness who, however, could not be contacted for further corroboration. Only in the remaining 14 percent of cases were there no witnesses who would have been able to confirm the perceptions of the NDEr. A full 88 percent of the cases confirmed by an independent witness were completely accurate, 10 percent contained some (often minor) error, and only 2 percent were completely erroneous.[8] Yet as impressive as it may sound, the quality of these data is weaker than that of the above-mentioned studies of Sabom and Sartori. It's the same problems all over: when it comes to individual case reports, memory errors of both the patient and the corroborating informant have to be accounted for—especially when interviewees (mostly family members of the NDEr) communicated with each other long before the interview took place, and a considerable amount of time has passed between the NDE and the interviews.

And then, there is a very human side to it: communal storytelling, story retelling, and with it, story embellishing. Such stories of wondrous "out-of-body" experiences are interesting. They are often moving. They seem to provide evidence for something miraculous happening near or at death—something beautiful, something heartwarming, something that most NDErs frequently experience as deeply spiritual, existential, reassuring.

And we bystanders need and relish such communal stories. Our social lives, our culture, and our understanding of the world are shaped by stories as much as our communal stories are shaped by our social lives, culture, and our understanding of the world. We live by and learn from such narratives; yet such narratives need not necessarily be accurate reports of events and facts. Sometimes they are parables, sometimes they are teaching tales, and sometimes they are accurate reports of what the NDEr experienced. Given the subjective nature and often unusual content of most NDEs (life reviews, "soul travel," encounters with otherworldly realms or beings), it can be very difficult to the outsider to decide which is which. The stories themselves rarely differ that much.

So perhaps for every report of veridical perception during an NDE that passes the test of being scrutinized and checked by third parties, there is probably at least one other story that becomes just a little more

exciting, a little more dramatic, and seemingly a little more eviden-
tially convincing with every telling. And, as memory research shows,
unfortunately, also a little less true:

> How one retells an event depends on the audience and the
> purpose of retelling. For example, when testifying in court
> or supplying evidence to a police officer, people usually try
> to be as accurate as possible. However, when relating an an-
> ecdote to friends, people often focus on entertaining their
> audience rather than on accuracy. In this case, they may
> make the story more interesting by omitting certain details
> and exaggerating and embellishing others. The act of retell-
> ing is a creative, constructive process, and the final product
> depends on the perspective the reteller adopts. For better or
> for worse, this perspective can affect what the reteller later
> remembers or misremembers.[9]

More than once I have heard such a wondrous and overwhelmingly convincing NDE story and halfway through the story had a sort
of déjà vu experience: only to soon wake up to the fact that I already
knew the story. I had already heard it last year; it had only been a little less sensational and evidential the first time I heard it. It's all too
human. And it is all too easy to understand—of course people want
to tell (and listen to) a good story, especially in view of the fact that
modern Western culture hasn't had many inspiring contemporary
death narratives to draw from. I myself and probably many of my colleagues enjoy such stories—perhaps as much as the one who is telling
them. But all this does not help to increase their evidential value.

There is much more to say about embellished NDE narratives and,
in particular, the unsettling tendency in some corners of the popular
NDE movement to give certain narratives disproportionately more
attention than others, while most other NDErs are never brought to

(nor seek) the attention of a broader public. Within the NDE movement, this has repeatedly led to individual NDErs claiming an almost prophet-like status for themselves, as if having an NDE bestowed one with special spiritual authority.[10] But why should that be so? All of us will die; all of us will have our very own personal death, and I doubt that my death experience will hold special lessons for you, or yours will hold special lessons for me. So, it is not always clear to me what exactly justifies the special status assigned to some NDErs. Whether it's due to special characteristics of the respective NDE (or its narrator), or whether it's perhaps due to more mundane reasons such as attention seeking and/or effective marketing. There is a tendency to satisfy the need (and market) for communal stories that are perhaps a little embellished here and there, a little more evidential, a little better, a little spicier, and unfortunately also a little less accurate, which is why we need to rely on systematic research work (such as Sabom's and Sartori's) rather than individual stories; and which is why we need many more such studies.

"A Genius When I Was Dead"

However, for our question of whether our conscious mind and self could potentially "outlive" a dysfunctional brain under the boundary or extreme condition of death and dying, there is another feature of the NDE that is perhaps less error-prone and yet no less relevant: namely less *what* people experience or claim to perceive during an NDE, but rather *whether* they experience anything at all and if so, *how* they experience it.

For that is precisely what is at issue here: Can we find further indications suggestive of the notion that, as Bruce Greyson suggests, under the extreme conditions of death and dying the usually observed dependence of our mental life on uncompromised brain function is

somehow "loosened"? Can self- and personhood, conscious experience, thinking, and memory unfold in the absence of their necessary
neurological basis, at least when we are close to death? If you ask
NDErs themselves, the answer appears to be in the affirmative. And
not only that—one frequently hears or reads reports that during near-
mortal crisis, NDErs were not only lucid, but could actually think
more clearly, logically, and faster than ever before; many also report
extraordinarily strong and vivid visual impressions. So, as paradoxical
as it sounds, to put it in the words of one of our study participants: "I
was a genius when I was dead."

For instance, a study with several hundred NDErs showed that
a full 80 percent of experiencers described their thinking during the
NDE as "clearer than usual" (45 percent) or "as clear as usual" (35 percent); furthermore, 65 percent recounted that their thinking during
the NDE was "as logical as usual" (36 percent) or "more logical than
usual" (29 percent).[11] Additionally, it has been shown that NDErs who
reported complex mentation and imagery during their NDE were
significantly more often close to death than those who did not,[12] meaning that in contrast to neurobiological models of mind and cognition,
the more severe the physiological crisis, the more likely are NDErs
to experience (or report experiencing) complex cognitive functioning.

{ 13 }

Mind, Memory, and Vision near Death

Thinking and Seeing near Death

When I decided, together with my students and members of my first informal research group on TL, to do our pilot study, and the surveys were sent out, we expected that we'd have to wait a long time until we received enough case reports. At the same time, we were admittedly impatient—the prospect of encountering a phenomenon both so unlikely and so philosophically, existentially, perhaps even spiritually significant made the waiting hardly bearable (although as noted earlier, case reports began to arrive the very next day, and in much larger numbers than we anticipated). During one of our research meetings, we therefore thought about similar phenomena we could study in parallel, in order to bridge the expected waiting time of the TL pilot study. Soon we came up with the idea to study lucidity and visual ability in persons who are not chronically ill (such as dementia and other neurologically impaired patients), but who nonetheless are undergoing a severe health crisis that also likely entails disturbance of normal brain function. Should Bruce's suggestion have merit—that near death, the strong dependence of mind on brain function may be loosened—we should expect to find similar phenomena in other death-related states, such as the NDE.

So we searched several scientific databases, only to see that very little research work had been conducted on the question of what to make of so many NDErs' claims of enhanced cognitive lucidity and visual imagery near death. We therefore decided to use the waiting time for conducting a study on precisely this issue. Little did we know that we'd soon be overwhelmed both with data on TL *and* on enhanced cognition and visual imagery near death.

For our study[1] we surveyed 653 NDE reports from several NDE databases that contained specific information about the medical context of the occurrence of the NDE. These reports indicated that experiencers were medically diagnosed as suffering from cardiac and/or respiratory arrest, and additionally included at least one explicit and unprompted reference to visual perception and/or imagery and higher cognition (i.e., "I saw the car wreck from about three meters above"; "I thought about my children. What would they do without me?").

We evaluated these accounts according to a simple scoring system, depending on whether the experiencers reported any change (or no such change) in either their visual ability or cognition (or both) during their cardiac or respiratory arrests. All references to visual perception or imagery and alertness or mentation were scored on scales between -2 (strongly impaired vision or cognition as compared to a typical day in everyday life); -1 (slightly impaired vision or cognition as compared to a typical day in everyday life); 0 (no difference noted or mentioned in either vision or cognition as compared to a typical day in everyday life); +1 (slightly enhanced vision or cognition as compared to a typical day in everyday life); and +2 (strongly enhanced vision or cognition as compared to a typical day in everyday life).

If a report referred to seeing or thinking, but did not include any additional descriptor or direct or indirect qualifier about the quality of seeing or thinking near death, but merely described seeing or thinking in comparable manner to everyday wakefulness, it was scored as 0. As is usual in studies in which several raters score reports, several test runs were necessary to establish a satisfactory rater agreement so that scoring was a function of the report's content, and not the generosity or strictness of the rater. Examples for each score in visual ability and cognition will be given below.

Study Results

Demographic information on age and gender was available for only 489 of all 653 subjects. The experiencers were aged eighteen to seventy-four (with a mean age of fifty-four), and 63 percent were female. Medical precursors of the NDE varied widely, and included, for example, clinical death not otherwise specified, surgery complications, organ failure, head injury, suicide attempts, anaphylactic shock, drowning or diving accidents, and car accidents. In the vast majority—504 (or 77 percent) of the whole sample—the NDE-related health crisis had a sudden onset and was not preceded by chronic life-threatening illness. The remaining 23 percent of the subjects indicated that they had been physically unwell for a longer period of time and/or had expected an impending deterioration of health status before their NDE-related crisis.

Seeing near Death

As to visual imagery during the NDE, out of the entire sample of 653 experiences, only forty-one accounts, or 6 percent, contained *no* explicit mention of any visual imagery, but instead primarily referred to feelings or thinking or spiritual insights gained during the NDE.

These forty-one accounts were therefore not scored on the visual imagery scale, leaving a large scorable visual imagery sample of 612 accounts.

Slightly less than half of these reports (252 or 41 percent of these
612) were scored 0, as the experiencers did mention visual experiences,
but the report did not indicate any change in visual quality compared
to everyday life. This doesn't sound particularly remarkable, yet think
of it: these NDErs suffered from cardiac or respiratory arrest, were
unconscious and near death, and yet "saw" just as normally as they did
before their cardiac and/or respiratory arrest:

> I saw that my dad and stepmom had a worried look on their
> faces and tried to ask why but they did not hear me.

> Though it was not normal to be dead, it felt very normal.
> The only difference was that I just heard the doctor calling
> "code blue" and it took me a while to figure out that he was
> referring to me (or rather my body).

> Given that I had just had a heart attack, I was very calm and
> collected and everything felt totally normal and natural. I
> was I. But my body was not I. I looked around and thought:
> "Wow, what a cold and ugly hospital room."

Only about a tenth of the sample (73 of 612, or 12 percent) indicated
that during at least one point in their NDE, their vision got worse.
Interestingly, however, in the majority of these seventy-three cases (84
percent), the experiencers attributed their diminished or lost vision to
their surroundings rather than to a loss or decline of vision per se:

> I had no vision; everything was dark.

> I could see nothing, it was complete darkness.

It was very dark, and I only saw some shadows in a distance, but could not recognize who they were.

Additionally, the majority of those who reported a temporarily diminished sense of vision later on indicated that as the experience unfolded, there was either a return of normal vision or a marked enhancement of visual imagery, such as when they experienced what appeared to them to be visually vivid scenery or encounters with deceased relatives, non-human persons, lights, and other visual images:

> I was in the midst of utter warm darkness, nothing, only nothing. I was unafraid, but it was total darkness and warmth. After a while, I saw a tiny little ray of light piercing the darkness, then two, then dozens of them, and soon found myself bathing in multicolored light rays. It was the most extraordinary thing I ever saw. Not only "seeing" it, actually, but living in it.

> In the beginning, I saw nothing. It was very dark. But it was not frightening . . . the most beautiful black I ever "saw." Then, suddenly, it was as if someone had switched on the lights. And what lights! Warm, peaceful, heartrendingly beautiful light that I saw with my heart, not my eyes. I long for that light every day.

Nearly half of the remaining 287 subjects (47 percent) reported either some (149 subjects, or 24 percent) or marked (139 subjects, or 23 percent) improvement of visual ability during their NDE:

> No need for glasses anymore! I saw perfectly well without them.

I sat up and was in awe at how clear everything appeared. I had worn glasses or contacts my entire life, so I was amazed at the sharpness of the room around me and the vividness of the colors. I could perceive an energy surrounding everything. The books, desk, furniture of the room all seemed to have a slight glow that radiated from them. No sooner had I noticed this than I realized I could see 360 degrees around me. I didn't need to turn my head, I just looked and I saw. There behind me lay my body and at that moment, I realized I had died.

I could clearly see my environment there, which is normally totally impossible for me to do without glasses. The colors were so much more intense and clear than on Earth.

I am normally very near-sighted and my glasses had been removed before surgery. But I was able to see things within the hospital as clearly as if I had my glasses on. When on the "other side," I was able to see with an intensity of color and range of vision that I had never before been able to do.

It was entirely different than "seeing" as you would define it. "Seeing" there is in entirety. The images were created in my knowing through great vibrations, all energy expressing itself through different frequencies. Light was used to send thoughts into me, that then formed images, but not before my eyes, in my mind as though I had seen it.

My eyesight was not very good before or after my wonderful experience, but during my experience, it was enormous. I saw every little crack on the wall of the hospital, I saw the tiniest spiders or flies in the corner of the windows, and they looked so so so beautiful! A web of life, everything alive deeply connected. I saw sparkles of life and light in and around these tiny creatures. I saw a tree in the hospital garden, and I didn't need to "move" closer to it to see each leaf, its structure, its veins. And then I saw a stone—must have been a normal pebble. But I saw every detail of it, its texture, its enormous beauty! And all of this from my hospital room, and without moving an inch closer to the hospital garden . . . it was a glorious time outside of my body!

My seeing had become very different. It was not normal "seeing," it was more like "sensing." I could perceive and understand every detail of the ER, and all at once! This was 4D seeing—one added dimension of color, clarity, substance, vibration!

Thinking near Death

As to the question of alertness and cognition during the NDE, only about a third (35 percent, or 226 accounts of the entire sample of 653 case reports) contained no explicit mention of cognitive processes during the experience. They were therefore not scored, even though the majority of these reports (about 85 percent or 191 of the 226 "cognition not mentioned" cases) contained references to often complex content that were suggestive of at least normal, if not enhanced cognitive functioning:

It was so beautiful but I also longed to be with my children. Leaving them alone at this early age seemed overwhelmingly painful.

I longed to tell my husband and my mother I was fine.

The remaining 427 reports contained explicit references to alertness and mentation, and only these could be scored according to the scoring scheme. Of these 427 case reports, only one single subject indicated a marked *decrease* of alertness and mentation:

> I just felt as if half asleep. Whenever "I woke up" during the time I was out of my body, I found the outlook of survival simply too tiring and not very exciting at all and fell back into what I would compare to a fitful half sleep.

And only three percent (thirteen subjects) reported what appeared to suggest a slight decline in thinking, but not in alertness:

> Very present and awake, but also extremely relaxed. My thinking was strangely viscous and slow.

> I simply wanted to watch this beautiful warm yellowish light. That is all. I simply watched, enjoying my "life" (death?) for the first time after the sad and painful weeks in hospital.

> I felt peaceful, receptive. Was totally empty, but in a very positive and elated way. "Finally I am at home"—I repeated over and over again like a mantra. Nothing much happened inside me. All happened out there and I watched and was happy, very, very happy.

> The journey felt like a dream. But it wasn't a dream and the feelings were extremely intense, but dreamy.

> It reminded me of my student days when we took acid: mind-blowing.

Two hundred and sixty-two subjects (61 percent of the scorable sample) mentioned being conscious of their self, their environments, and thinking, but did not use any further qualifying adjectives or any indication of either decline or enhancement of the scored dimension (meaning these were scored 0—no change):

> Here I was, very surprised to be awake! I wondered whether this meant that I was dead or whether I was experiencing the effects of some medication given to me by the MDs.

The remaining 151 subjects (35 percent of the scorable group) reported either slight (seventy subjects or 16 percent) or marked (eighty-one subjects or 19 percent) heightening of awareness and alertness and clearer thinking:

> I felt extremely aware, totally present, sharp, and focused. In hindsight, it's like being half asleep when I was alive, and totally awake after I was pronounced dead.

> My mind felt cleared and my thoughts seemed quick and decisive. I felt a great sense of freedom and was quite content to be rid of my body. I felt a connection with everything around me in a way that I cannot describe. I felt as if I was thinking faster or that time had slowed down considerably.

> During this I remembered everything in my life, with all the details and very accurately, everything since my birth till the time of the accident. I remembered all the people I knew, even the ones whom I met only once or twice. I remembered all the events, the important and nonimportant ones when my age was less than a year. I remembered it

with all its details. It passed in front of me and I saw it as a cinema show in just fifteen minutes. When I got out of the car I was in full consciousness. I felt that I wasn't in the car, or in other words, I was existing and not existing, a feeling that is difficult to describe.

While I was unconscious at the accident scene, I was hovering above the entire scene below and looking down. I saw the car against the tree, and the ambulance as well as onlookers from the neighborhood and stopped cars. I was in no danger and no pain. I was perfectly aware of what was going on below me in a state of complete tranquility. There was no discomfort, no judgment, and no concerns. My soul left my body and was in a heightened state of consciousness. Ironically, even though I was "unconscious," my soul was more alert and aware than it could have been merged with my body and mind.

They put me in the ambulance and we were off. My husband followed the ambulance. He later told me he was crying so hard while driving he didn't know how he did it. I was losing consciousness in the ambulance but I thought "hold on" with all my strength. I felt I was slipping away fast. The next thing I noticed I was without pain. More alert, my mind had never been clearer or more alive than at that moment.

More consciousness and alertness than normal. I was much more alert and much smarter! Maybe a little too smart because I argued with Jesus to let me stay! I just felt better mentally and physically altogether.

While I was floating above, I was more alert and conscious than I can ever remember being.

More consciousness and alertness than normal. I'd have to say that I was more alert only because I was experiencing the presence of celestial beings and had gained clarity on death. Otherwise, I was just as alert as any other regular moment in my life.

I was expanded, both in my feeling and in my thinking. It was not head versus heart, both being high-functional—higher than I ever experienced during my normal life. And I remembered all. Every day of my life, every conversation, and every word—every word!—of books I had read, and I had read a lot, though I had not read anything that would have prepared me for my NDE. But I remembered poems I had not thought about for twenty or thirty years. When I later checked whether I had remembered them correctly, it turned out I had. *There must be a second memory store somewhere in the universe, and I was accessing it without the slightest effort.* I was totally clear, totally aware, and totally calm.

Knowledge was given. I guess that is why I felt more alert. It was like a flash drive and my entire life and family were plugged into me and downloaded. The knowledge I gained held answers to everything. So in that sense I was enlightened?

When I entered the light, I noted something very interesting. I knew that my normal, old me would be overwhelmed. It would have simply been too much. But now I understand something very profound. I was raised to a new level of thinking and feeling so that I could encounter this light and not be totally overwhelmed. My thinking was faster, my feelings were more complex and differentiated, and my overall state was lucid. I thought about the "new creation"

mentioned in the bible, or the body of light. It was more like
a mind of light, though.

I was very alert, sharp, focused, and clear. My thought was
much faster than usual, and more logical. Thinking was a bit
like observing an immensely fine-tuned and complex machine processing an immense amount of data, and providing
me with the answer. It was as if my brain had changed into a
supercomputer. Crazy as it sounds, but I was a genius when
I was dead. And I never was as awake as on the day I died.
Crazy, no?

To summarize the results of this study on yet another extreme condition of brain and mind (being near death with cardiac and/or respiratory arrest), we found additional support for the notion that a
substantial number of subjects spontaneously reported either normal
and often enhanced visual imagery during their NDE. Secondly, we
found that the majority of subjects recounted either normal or enhanced alertness, memory, and logical thinking during their NDE. To
the outside observer, however, these patients were unconscious and in
most cases, barely alive.

The findings of this study therefore align well both with what we
find in TL (heightened cognition and mental function during compromised brain function when close to death) and more generally the
notion that under the boundary or extreme conditions of the brain-
mind relationship, brain-mind materialism no longer applies. Or so it
looks like at face value.

{ 14 }

Relating the NDE and TL

Overlaps and Differences Between TL and the NDE

Given this study and the reports, it is time for a brief reflection and stocktaking of what we know and don't know about the fate of our minds—ourselves—at and near death. We have on the one hand the reports of those who witnessed TL; they are hard to dismiss and the numbers of such reports are growing steadily. And we have what seems to be corroborating indications of similarly enhanced cognition and visual imagery during the NDE.

In assessing the evidence, however, the question remains whether it indeed suggests that a conscious self and mind can somehow "outlive" or continue to function in the face of brain dysfunction—at least close to death. Did we find white crows or mere anecdotes and memory errors?

As we will soon see, this question leads us back to TL—because as is so often the case when we try to understand complex and ambiguous cases and findings, it is not solely *individual* pieces of evidence that

decide whether a plausible case can be made for a notion, but also the
question of whether several pieces of circumstantial evidence support
each other. To connect the dots, you need several of them; one does
not suffice.

To do this, finding and analyzing the potential weaknesses of individual data points is usually a good starter. Doing so not only allows
us to take an honest and unbiased stock of the available evidence; it also
tells us what we need to keep looking for in order to assess whether
these weaknesses are compensated for or strengthened by other findings. As to the weaknesses, the two major ones of our NDE study
are: (a) the lingering uncertainty as to when exactly during the medical
crisis the NDE occurs (I will come to that in a moment), and (b) the fact
that the NDE, like every personal experience, is deeply subjective—
that is, the evidential value of our study results (and similar claims of
enhanced cognition and visual imagery during the NDE) stands or falls
not least with the question of how much we are willing to believe the respondents of our study. Were their visual impressions really more vivid,
more intense, and stronger than in their healthy everyday state? Was
cognition really clearer than ever before, their thinking more logical,
their comprehension faster, their memory better?

Precisely because of its potentially wide-ranging implications, we
need to take a closer and more critical look at this point and consider,
for example, the limits of self-assessment of cognitive functions and one's
own state of consciousness. Unfortunately, there is a large body of research that suggests that people often are not particularly skilled at judging their own cognitive state. The explanation is simple: judging one's
own cognitive state is itself a higher cognitive operation that requires
considerable self-awareness and cognitive capacity to begin with.[1] Ask a
drunken person how well he or she functions, and he or she may tell you
that all is fine, he or she is able to run a machine, drive a car, understand
complex subject matters, and in fact feels very competent and confident,

thank you. But then look at and assess actual performance, and you'd quickly remove him or her from the driver's seat, the machine, and steer the conversation to less complex subject matters. So how valid are the claims of our NDErs that they were more lucid and attentive, had clearer and more logical thinking than in their everyday lives? It's a tricky question. Though we have little to no clinical or empirical data on self-assessment of lucidity during the NDE, we do know that the NDE is an intense spiritual experience and that our ability to self-assess tends to be compromised in such states of high affective arousal.

"What's a Mistake but a Kind of Take?": *William James, Intoxicated*

One of the better-known literary examples of this problem can be found in William James's notes on his philosophical experiments with nitrous oxide, used during his era as a narcotic in dentistry. In addition to its analgesic properties, nitrous oxide also exerts a dose-dependent psychedelic effect, and William James, ever interested in studying the limits of the human mind, consumed it occasionally in order to experience "profound mystical insights into the nature of the universe"— including the ability to understand Hegel's idealistic philosophy ("it made me understand better than ever before both the strength and the weakness of Hegel's philosophy"):

> I strongly urge others to repeat the experiment, which with pure gas is short and harmless enough. [. . .] With me, as with every other person of whom I have heard, the keynote of the experience is the tremendously exciting sense of an intense metaphysical illumination. Truth lies open to the view in depth beneath depth of almost blinding evidence. The

mind sees all the logical relations of being with an apparent subtlety and spontaneity to which its normal consciousness offers no parallel.[2]

So much so that James eventually felt the urge to write down his insights gained under the influence of nitrous oxide. But when he later read his notes, all that was left behind were unintelligible "tattered fragments" that must have seemed to an outside observer, James wrote, like "meaningless drivel but which at the moment of transcribing were fused in the fire of infinite rationality":

> What's a mistake but a kind of take?
> What's nausea but a kind of-usea?
> Sober, drunk,-unk, astonishment.
> Everything can become the subject of criticism—
> How criticize without something to criticize?
> Agreement—disagreement!!
> Emotion—motion!!!!
> By God, how that hurts! By God, how it doesn't hurt!
> Reconciliation of two extremes.
> By George, nothing but othing!
> That sounds like nonsense, but it is pure onsense!
> Thought deeper than speech . . . !
> Medical school; divinity school, school! SCHOOL!
> Oh my God, oh God; oh God!

The most coherent and articulate sentence was this: "There are no differences but differences of degree between different degrees of difference and no difference."[3]

So much or so little remained of the ostensibly incredibly lucid and mystical experience of and insights into cosmic consciousness experi-

enced by intoxicated William James. Although James, in his beautiful essay "Subjective Effects of Nitrous Oxide," ultimately comes to a
somewhat more benevolent assessment of the insights gained during
nitrous oxide intoxication, his is not the only case in which the self-
assessment of one's state and the insights gained during a spiritual or
mystical experience turn out to be frustratingly unreliable. How then
do we know whether at least some of the reports by our subjects that
their thinking was more logical, faster, in fact "genius" aren't equally
unreliable? The truth is: we do not, for the fact remains that the self-
assessment of "clear and logical thinking" or expansion of consciousness comes to its limits precisely because one must first be clear and
logical oneself in order to judge whether one is really thinking clearly
or more clearly and logically in a given situation.

Memory and Vision and the NDE

But there are other aspects of enhanced cognition during the NDE
that can be verified externally, and that tend to support the notion that
at least some of the subjects did truly experience enhanced mental
capacity during their crisis: visual imagery and memory. A large number of NDErs (in our study and other research work as well) note that
during their NDE, they not only had the impression of being able
to think faster and clearer, but that they also were able to remember
long-forgotten events (often with minute detail) and facts:

> My memory was vast. I remembered everything, each lit-
> tle detail of my class rooms (thirty years ago!), the faces and
> names of my school teachers, every word I had written in my
> student assignments, every book I had read, what I wore on
> which day. It was all there again.

It's important to note that in a number of cases, upon subsequent checking on the veracity of these memories, it turned out that these memories were true and not merely imagined or false memories:

> I knew things I didn't think I knew. Perhaps I had forgotten what I knew, but for example my memory was astounding. I later checked on a few of the episodes I remembered by going through my parents' photo album and confirmed these memories.

Thus we find that just the aspect—memory—of the claimed enhanced cognition during the NDE that is in principle reasonably verifiable stands up to scrutiny—at least within the bounds of what is verifiable in such cases. Certainly and without question, further studies are needed to shed more light on this aspect; but at least in view of the data available so far, there is some weak evidence that enhanced cognition and memory during the NDE is not solely based on erroneous self-assessments.

Secondly, there were the many reports of enhanced visual imagery during the NDE, and it seems as if these reports are much less affected by the problem of the limits of self-assessment. One may err about how lucid and rational one is or was at a given time, one may err about the accuracy of one's memories—but it is far less likely to err about how clearly or well one saw or processed visual impressions at a given moment (also note that there were significantly more reports that visual imagery was much finer, improved, clearer, and enhanced during the NDE: in 83 percent of our sample).

So what is the overall assessment of our findings? On the one hand, as the example of William James (and numerous studies on metacognition) illustrates, there are clear limits to subjective assessments of one's cognitive abilities. Thus, if self-assessment of cognitive abilities during NDEs were all we had to go on, it would not be much. On the other hand, there are aspects (visual imagery and verifiable memory) that are not as prone to error as the assessment of one's own rationality and thinking ability, and it so happens that both visual imagery and memory enhancement were frequently mentioned by our subjects— more frequently in fact than thinking ability and general lucidity.

Bridging the Gap

Nevertheless, the fact that the NDE is a purely subjective experience somewhat weakens the evidential value of these findings; we still have to take our study participants' words for it. And so it will remain unless we encounter other phenomena that can tip the balance either way and support or weaken these reports—for example, because the lucidity reported by the respondents can be confirmed by outside witnesses, preferably in real time, and not only, as is the case for the memory verifications, at a later time.

There remains the lingering doubt that we do not know when exactly the NDE occurs—although there are a very few studies (Sabom and Sartori) that at least provide some indication that apparently some NDErs may have had their NDE at the time when they were clinically dead and underwent CPR. In short—some major uncertainties and weaknesses remain, and we would need to seek further complementary findings to add to the evidential value of the NDE.

But here is the crucial point: we no longer have to search for such a complementary and corroborating phenomenon—we already have found it: TL. TL in fact is beset with *none* of the weaknesses that beset our NDE data: we know *exactly* when TL takes place. In contrast to the NDE, TL is observed in real time, "live" if you will. And as much as the NDE is a private experience that no one from the outside can have access to—with all uncertainties and ambiguities coming with private experiences—TL is a public event. We *only* know about it because and when witnesses are present who note and observe the patient's unexpected lucidity near death. The return of cognitive ability, responsive and intelligent speech, and biographical and declarative memory is observed and confirmed by these witnesses—it is the key feature of TL.

The findings from TL research thus complement and support our NDE data and vice versa: TL data offer a third-person perspective window, and the NDE data a first-person perspective on mind at death. Furthermore, once we established that near death unexpected psychological phenomena can occur, both the TL and NDE data may also cast light on the findings of the few studies cited above regarding perception during an NDE and mindsight in the blind during an NDE.

So at this point, we have two sets of data—TL, and cognitive and visual enhancement during the NDE—and a proposal, namely Bruce Greyson's suggestion that the everyday complete dependence of the mind on brain function may no longer fully hold at the "extreme" or boundary condition of death and dying. But with that, the questions don't end. They actually begin. What does this mean? How can we possibly make sense of all of this?

15

Making Sense of It

After the Eclipse

At this point, I should like to introduce an analogy that I owe to my friend and colleague, Israeli physicist and philosopher Avshalom Elitzur. Years ago, we met in Alpbach—a beautiful village (in fact, frequently and deservedly voted to be one of Austria's most beautiful and romantic villages) in the Tyrolean Mountains and home of the Forum Alpbach, a regular meeting of scientists, philosophers, and the odd politician to meet and discuss and imagine ways to rehumanize and nourish our quest for a just and sustainable society. During this summer meeting, we were taking long walks up in the mountains. And on the rainy days, we'd stay in the car, up in the mountains, windows or doors open, literally breathing in the summer rain and dew from the mountain firs, the songs of the birds mixing with sitar music from the car's tape recorder, while we discussed and shared our respective ideas, insights, and questions on mind, the brain, and—Avshalom's main field—physics, time, and consciousness.

Fittingly, we ended most of our walks at the cemetery of Alpbach—to visit and pay tribute to one of Alpbach's most famous former inhabitants, Erwin Schrödinger (the author of two pillars of quantum mechanics: the Schrödinger equation and Schrödinger's cat paradox, and—lesser known—the developer of a non-reductionist, "universal mind" theory of selfhood).

Avshalom had recently published a widely discussed article in the *Journal of Consciousness Studies* in which he "reluctantly confessed" that he had stumbled upon a compelling argument (too complex to be discussed here) for brain-mind dualism,[1] yet was somewhat "embarrassed" that he, as a physicist, would end up arguing for dualism, meaning the inclusion of something "immaterial" (such as conscious minds) in the fabric of the world. As an outcome of our discussions, Avshalom and I eventually edited two volumes on consciousness— discussing why both of us strongly doubted that it would ever be possible to explain consciousness in purely material terms.

All of this happened long before I even heard of TL, but had already conducted my earlier quoted interview with Sir John C. Eccles on dualism, the self, and Eccles's view that the self is not a product of the brain; that it is not a biological entity at all. And indeed, Avshalom's views expressed in his articles corresponded largely to Sir John C. Eccles's classical dualist proposal that we are twofold beings, not only at death and dying, but throughout our entire life; that we have physical properties because we have a material body and that we have (or, rather, are) non-material self-conscious minds ("souls," if you will) in addition to the physical body.

This kind of dualism is of course not a new model; most spiritual and wisdom traditions, and most religions, hold that there is something about our being that cannot be captured in purely biological or material terms. That there is a soul, and that it is the soul that counts— remember the story of Socrates' death quoted at the beginning of this book: "We must care for it [the soul], not only in respect to this time, that we call life, but in respect to all time."

But if dualism is true, why then don't we find souls when we look for them in the brain? Why do we rather find, at least in everyday life, a self that seems to be so utterly dependent on what is happening to and in our brains? Why only at death or other very special circumstances (parts of which were also at the core of Avshalom's "reluctant dualism") do we find evidence of something more? To understand this point, Avshalom came up with an analogy that I find particularly useful in this context. According to Avshalom, the everyday mind-brain relationship resembles a total solar eclipse—the moon fully covers the sun, and the only traces of the sun you see are the coronal filaments ("rays"). If we didn't know better, there would be prima facie no compelling reason to propose the existence of a sun (soul) behind the moon (brain). For the sake of explanatory simplicity (a prime scientific virtue), we'd say that we see one body, and have no reason to suggest that there are two. We'd probably suspect that the moon has an aura of filaments that, though poorly understood at the moment, would one day be explicable by as yet undiscovered properties of the moon's surface (materialism). Study the moon, and the filaments will be understood in due course. Study the brain, and there'll be no need at all to posit an autonomous conscious self.

On the face of it, there is nothing wrong with this approach. On the contrary—one general rule in rational discourse is not to unduly inflate the number of variables, unless it turns out that there is an absolute need for adding new variables—such as new research findings, newly observed phenomena that don't fit into our former explanatory framework (moon only/brain only). So, if under normal conditions, we always detect brain activity along with mental activity, why assume that mental activity is not in fact brain activity ("First, you take away the soul. There is no place for souls in science.")?

But what if we encounter phenomena such as cognitive enhancement during the NDE or TL? Such findings will be met with skepticism—just as the NDE and TL were—until and unless the sheer number of such reports will make alternative explanations such as confabulation, fraud, false memories, and other factors increasingly unlikely. But then, what do we see? And what will we conclude? According to Avshalom, such cases largely corresponded to what happens when the eclipse subsides. When the moon makes possible the view of the sun behind it, we see, for the first time, direct evidence suggestive of the idea that there are in fact two celestial bodies and not one. And only when the self shines through beyond the brain at the hour of death, do we have direct indications that it might after all not be a product of the enchanted loom. And only then can we see that another model—such as dualism—can account both for the sunbeams visible during the eclipse and the full view of two celestial bodies after the eclipse is over. This type of dualism of self and brain thus corresponds most closely to what we associate with the classical concept of the soul as the nonmaterial source and center of our personal identity and selfhood. According to this model, body and soul are in an intimate reciprocal relationship—just how intimate this relationship is, is demonstrated not least by the devastating consequences of dementia and other severe neurological disorders on our experience, thinking, and behavior. At the same time, the autonomy and independence of the mind becomes apparent under more extreme circumstances such as death and dying—i.e., when the eclipse comes to an end.

The Soul, Mind at Large

A related, yet slightly different model is equally capable of accounting for our findings. It was advocated by the French philosopher and Nobel laureate in literature Henri Bergson, the Cambridge philosopher

C. D. Broad, Oxford philosopher Ferdinand Schiller, and William James, and popularized by Aldous Huxley—and incidentally closely resembles Schrödinger's theory of consciousness. According to this idea, there exists a Mind at Large, a huge reservoir or ocean of consciousness and knowledge—and each of us is a part of it, potentially aware of our connection with everything. But to be able to function in everyday life, to be and develop as individuals, the primary function of the brain and nervous system is to protect us from being overwhelmed and confused by this vast ocean of conscious experience. In this view, then, the brain is not generating conscious experience and the self; rather it is shutting out most of what we don't need for, and that would in fact distract us from, everyday survival:

> [. . .] But insofar as we are animals, our business is at all costs to survive. To make biological survival possible, Mind at Large has to be funneled through the reducing valve of the brain and nervous system. What comes out at the other end is a measly trickle of the kind of consciousness that will help us to stay alive on the surface of this particular planet.[2]

Accordingly, this model assumes that the brain works primarily as an eliminative, i.e., inhibitory, organ for consciousness, filtering out from the variety of potential conscious experiences only those that are mandatory and useful at a given time for immediate biological survival. The brain would thus be, as Bergson puts it, "the organ of attention to life," a "reducing valve," actively involved in inhibiting, constricting, and eliminating a potentially much greater and expanded consciousness. And yet, traces of this expanded consciousness can be experienced in moments of deep meditation, prayer, altered states induced by certain psychedelic (or "mind-expanding") substances, perhaps also during the NDE, and at times when we are simply receptive and spend a day in nature. Then, the floodgates open—in such cases,

the organism's inhibitory functions are lowered, consciousness un-
folds, expands, reconnects to Mind at Large.

The brain-as-filter theory was not originally developed to explain
the effects of neurological diseases on our individual minds and consciousness, or even phenomena such as TL. But the filter theory would
be just as suitable as classical dualism in helping us to understand
heightened and expanded consciousness in previously cognitively impaired patients near death. When the filter breaks down, consciousness is not eliminated, but "released"—which might also help us make
sense of the fact that so many NDErs tell us that during their NDE,
their consciousness was vast, cosmic, all-encompassing. And that wak-
ing everyday life—"when I am back in the body," as they sometimes
tell us—is comparatively dull and inhibited.

Dualism and the filter theory would render the strong dependence
of mental on neuronal functions just as plausible as their relative independence under certain circumstances near death. And there are other
models, too, that can account for these findings—I shall list some of
them here for readers who intend to further delve into this topic, such
as idealism, panpsychism, and some variants of non-reductive double-
aspect theories.

All of them are of course still highly speculative (as is materialism),
which is why I would like to intentionally leave it open at this point
how a concrete model that accommodates both clinical experience and
our TL and NDE findings could and should look like. My aim here
is not to present a full-blown dualist theory of the brain-mind relationship, but rather to show that it is possible to accommodate TL and
NDE lucidity without giving up the hope to find a testable model of
brain and mind, and who we are.[3]

In the research work described in the earlier chapters, I merely tried
to come closer to a better understanding of the nature of our self and
personhood by looking at and following its fate precisely at the junction where materialism and dualism make diametrically opposed pre-

dictions about its destiny: the point when the mechanics of the brain's "enchanted loom" (Sherrington) begin to fail and the self is virtually left to its own devices without a sufficiently functioning neural machinery.

Even without a full-blown theory of the self, I note that what we have found at this junction is not what materialism would have predicted: we found a sheltered, preserved self—preserved against all biological odds. A self, a mind that does not fade away into oblivion, but in the case of TL finds its way back to itself—and in the case of the NDE, sometimes appears to blossom even more than it ever did during everyday life. This research—though still only in its infancy and, I hope, the beginning of a new and open-ended debate about the nature and value of human personhood—consequently suggests that the self is indeed more than the product of that loom; that the loom is enchanted because the spirit of the weaver is at work in it.

PART IV

Person, Death, and Meaning

Every experience of beauty points to eternity.

—Hans Urs von Balthasar

16

A Sheltered Self

Incomprehensible Beauty, Unconditional Dignity

We have come a long way. And again and again we have found clues and hints that supported what Sir John C. Eccles had told me many, many years ago when I was just at the beginning of my academic career:

> I should like to add that to me, only one thing remains important. It is the mystery of our conscious self. [. . .] How does it come into being? What is its future destiny? [. . .] I think we simply have to acknowledge that there is a mystery, transcending any biological or materialist rationale, inherent to our existence.

As became clear in the last chapter, we still don't know much yet about the mystery of our conscious self. All that we have found are traces of its transcending the biological or materialist rationale. We encountered a sheltered, individual, and irreplaceable and unique self—a self that, precisely through the "return" of its unique memories and individuality, makes it known to those gathering around them that it (again) has access to its very own private memories and experiences that were previously thought to be lost, and with it, personal identity and individuality.

Many of our NDErs corroborate this. And they also bear witness to the relevance of our life stories, each chapter, each moment. They tell us, for example, that no detail, no encounter, no experience in this self's biography seems too insignificant to not be included in their life reviews. No decision is too trivial, no word too casual not to have had an influence on the lives of others in one way or another:

> Then my whole life. Every single second, flashed before my eyes at what seemed like light speed, but I still was able to comprehend everything. Not just every event, but every interaction I'd ever had. I saw how my words and actions had affected the recipients and what they had thought of me, good or bad.

> The next thing I knew, I was in darkness watching a detailed review of my life up to that point. It was like watching a huge cinema screen in 3D and it was incredibly detailed in that it, literally, covered every event in my life. I remembered events, people, and places that I had long forgotten. It was as if I was effectively reliving my entire life although it was done at high speed.

> I could see every part of my life, every event and incident all at once. Although it seemed instantaneous, I knew that every

moment was there. These days, I might say that I downloaded my whole hard drive. At the time, I think I tried to compare it to a replay of a cassette tape in fast forward.

At that point, I was totally unconcerned with whether I was alive or not. My focus was on what was being shown to me. A sort of film reel was directly in front of me but up just a bit. It was like watching an immense, very clear TV. I was watching images of every event that had taken place in my life. My entire life, all in pictures. The most interesting part of it was that with each picture, with all the pictures (there were more than I could count), I re-experienced the original feelings that had accompanied each one. And this was happening all at the same time! I could actually see my life in picture form and feel the emotion or the lesson in each one! All together and in complete unison. It was the most phenomenal experience! Not at all like we experience life. Here, you see a picture, for example, a photograph, and you have a memory. Then you pick up another picture and have another memory. But in this experience, I received complete knowledge of all my life events in picture form, reliving each picture's memory at the same moment! I have never forgotten what it was like to have the ability to relate to my life that way. Everything was so clear, so vivid!

I had learnt so much. How big an impact my seemingly small actions had on a large scale. How my choices and be-havior rippled through the lives of countless others. How the love I showed spread like wildfire. How the way I mis-treated others deeply hurt and affected them and also how that pain, fear, and confusion would then impact the lives of others too. In the "time" I spent in this reliving, I developed a deep gratitude for many things. The experience of life for one. The people and the hearts that had touched my soul in beautiful ways and the fragility of being human.

These reports converge with what TL seems to tell us: that the person, together with his or her biography, is not only biologically but also otherwise represented and preserved in ways that are hardly comprehensible at present. We can only speculate about the reasons for this enormously generous protection of our biography and identity and how it aligns with Eccles's proposal:

> that in our existence and in our experiences in life there is a great mystery that cannot be explained in a materialist way. This remainder that is left behind after everything else has been explained is, beyond all else, the final and decisive value of our world.[1]

So even if we currently lack a full-blown theory of the self at death, our studies and the stories of our research participants convey an important message. It is the message that life seems to have accorded so much value and significance to our individual existence and experiences that each and every one of us along with our personal biographies—you and I and the people we love—are not merely anchored in or "entrusted" to an object as fragile and vulnerable as our brain, but are also sheltered and preserved in a dimension of mind (Mind at Large?) that is as yet scarcely understood. Just as the NDEr whose report was reprinted on page 183 said:

> There must be a second memory store somewhere in the universe, and I was accessing it without the slightest effort.

Admittedly, at present we have not the slightest idea at all how it is even possible that our individual selfhood could be, to all appearances, guarded, protected, and made whole again at the end of life. Nor do we know why. And yet all of this also has strong and significant implications for the dignity of the person—a dignity that life itself appears to have placed in and woven into our very humanity. Think about it: something about us must have so much value and meaning, after all, that nature may have installed its own mechanism that allows our identity and memories to be preserved and sheltered even through illness, disease, and decline.

Care for the Soul

And if we acknowledge that much, then we've come back full circle to Socrates' last instructions to his students quoted at the beginning of this book. For it then follows that we have certain duties toward this self and other selves; and that we should nourish the self so that we may not only relish the fact that it is sheltered, but also are aware that what will remain of and with this self largely depends on us and our daily conduct. If nothing is really lost, should we not bear responsibility for that which is preserved? Will it not become part of history? Ours and the world's? This was Socrates' last teaching to his students:

> But now . . . the soul [. . .] cannot escape from evil or be saved in any other way than by becoming as good and wise as possible. For the soul takes with it to the other world nothing but its education and nurture, and these are said to benefit or injure the departed greatly from the very beginning of his journey thither.

Socrates' advice was to care for the soul, to nurture it, and to bring out the best parts possible in our dispositions, so that our story, our contribution to the history of the world is a chapter that is worth preserving, and not a trail of devastation, selfishness, unkindness, disinterest, and lack of benevolence toward others. According to Socrates (and to most wisdom traditions and religions), being a sheltered self is, among other things, also a source of moral obligation; it has to be cared for by ourselves and by others (and should take care of itself and others) just as one cares for certain valuable and precious "things" once one has sufficient reason to believe that they exist, even if one does not see them (for example, caring for people who are in need in faraway places even if one has never met them; or for animals and plants that are vulnerable and affected by one's actions, but that one has not yet directly encountered).

The question of the fate and future of the self, therefore, is anything but specious; rather, it is, as Socrates pointed out on his last day, a key question of how we live our lives. And as Socrates made clear, echoing no doubt the wisdom of earlier religious traditions he drew from: being a self is not only about who we *are*, but also about who we *become*. This is where, according to most wisdom teachings throughout the ages, the care for the soul begins, and ends: what we do with ourselves, others, and the world. Whether and how we realize and actualize our potential, our individuality, our personhood. In this context, I distinctly remember sitting in one of Viktor Frankl's last lectures (he was ninety years old) at Vienna Medical School. When asked about the concept of self-realization, he thought for a moment, and then he answered:

> Yes, but please do not realize everything that lays dormant
> in your self. Please realize only those aspects that are worthy
> and deserving of realization.

One sometimes reads, for example, that Socrates, as a young man, soon became aware of the fact that he had a high intelligence, quick perception, and rhetorical talent. And so he pondered the choice of becoming a cunning trickster who could easily twist the citizens of Athens around his finger, or whether he would put his abilities to the service of knowledge and become a wisdom teacher and philosopher. We know what Socrates chose: he did not blindly realize what talents—good and bad—lay dormant in him, but he made a choice.

Our NDErs, too, tell us unanimously that it is these conscious decisions that count—and will continue to count; for it is also these conscious decisions that make us who we are and what we one day will look back on when it is time to review our own lives: care for the soul, they tell us, the self, your life. And if you bring forth your best self, you will soon understand our best is never the best of us alone, but for others, too. That we should not only do everything to feel good, as modern consumer society wants to tell us; the question is also what we are good for. So, care for others in need, care for the world. Don't get lost in the hassles of everyday life without at least occasionally reminding yourself that your history, and the history of those around us, might well be vastly larger than what meets the eye.

I hope that I have been able to show in this book that we have good reason to again hope and believe that our existence is greater than what we see with the naked eye and that each of us, as John C. Eccles said, is embedded in a higher context, that our life is a meaningful adventure that is wonderfully protected and preserved. Just by having become a self, we are therefore enormously gifted—called into a life by a promise that we may not fully grasp yet. In return, *our* gift to life is that we perceive, realize, and live its meaning. For this, we bear responsibility.

17

Why It Matters

Honoring a Legacy

In this book, I tried to honor the legacy of three outstanding teachers who, as a young student in the 1990s, I had the good fortune to learn from—John C. Eccles, Viktor E. Frankl, Elisabeth Kübler-Ross—who encouraged, indeed called upon, a generation of students and future researchers, to never give up the belief in the inalienable dignity, freedom, and responsibility of the human being. Never to see the human being only as a complex and wonderful machine—but still only a machine—but as a unique and singular person.

All three were also witnesses of what can happen when humanity abandons faith in itself—in its own dignity and the dignity of others, especially the sick and the old and the weak. The twentieth century was a century of ideologies that despised human dignity; that decidedly did not take care of the soul, but "first took it away." What these teachers taught us about the moral and historical implications of reductionism and nihilism had a strong impact on us students who were fortunate enough to experience these and other researchers of the older generation personally in the lecture hall. Theirs was the credibility of those who had seen with their own eyes or even, like Frankl, suffered themselves what happens when humanity no longer appreciates the importance, dignity, uniqueness, and value of the human spirit (Frankl survived four concentration camps, and almost his entirely family was murdered during the Holocaust). And it was the generation that saw how much depends on the individual himself—even when fate (or even worse, other people) try to rob the human being of its inborn dignity. But these witnesses also taught us: one cannot take away this dignity from man; one can only deny man his dignity in ideological delusion. And still, he cannot and will not lose it. It is inalienably woven into our being a person, and with it, our personal responsibility. Frankl therefore writes, with a view to the three years he spent in the concentration camps:

> Our generation is realistic, for we have come to know man as he really is. After all, man is that being who invented the gas chambers of Auschwitz; however, he is also that being who entered those gas chambers upright, with the Lord's Prayer or the Shema Yisrael on his lips.[1]

But generations are now growing up who can no longer hear this testimony firsthand. They no longer hear the warning that the past century showed us, as Frankl put it—first, what man is capable of (Auschwitz), nor second, what is at stake (Hiroshima). And yet these present generations, like every generation before them, face the same questions: What is, who is man? What is he meant to be and to become? Does his—does my—life have meaning, a deeper significance, a greater destiny, or is my self merely a fleeting specter of self-awareness, ultimately destined for and embedded in a great nothingness? Recall the sad lines that Louie Savva wrote:

> We are all an end product and [. . .] I do not think I make
> a difference in the universe [. . .]. There is no point to life.[2]

Or David Lindley's terse discussion piece on the question of man's place in the cosmos, published in no less a mass medium as *USA Today*—an unceremonious swan song to human dignity and value:

> We humans are just crumbs of organic matter clinging to
> the surface of one tiny rock. Cosmically, we are no more sig-
> nificant than mold on a shower curtain.[3]

Such voices count. They have an impact. Their cynicism harms a world that needs nothing more urgently than the willingness to acknowledge that every human being counts, that our efforts are worthwhile, that we are sheltered and preserved, that we are not merely complex machines, but that our choices make a difference as to what and who is preserved—not only for our individual lives, but for the world at large. Think of the nine million people—nine million individual selves—who will starve to death this year; or the 350,000 children who will go blind this year due to malnutrition—even though we have the abilities and capacities to prevent it. Or think of the misery not only in poorer countries, but also in the midst of the inner neglect and emptiness in the rich industrial nations: the empty looks of those who are caught in routine, feelings of meaninglessness, alienation, cynicism. Think of how we treat ourselves, each other, nature, this world. And then think about what our discussions so far told us about who we really are, how much nature and life invest in us and our preservation. None of this is happening in a vacuum. For if *we* don't care about life, if we "take away the soul first," and if a person matters no more "than mold on a shower curtain"—yes, then that hope is truly in vain. Not because it has to be in vain, but because we have fallen for nihilism's ostensible self-fulfilling prophecy that this hope is in vain.

Rehabilitating Hope

But in fact, our generation harbors a great distrust of their own hopes, including their own hopes for a reality beyond the merely physical. It is possible—and is discussed in research on psychology and the history of ideas—that our postmodern age has developed a skepticism, or aversion to the spiritual, to values and idealism, however justified (usually not very rationally); and to the same extent has lost confidence in the viability of these values and of transcendence, including our own transcendent self. The contemporary values crisis often manifests itself in the form of a deep distrust of any notion of meaning and values, of the imperishable, the good, the beautiful, and the true, and of dignity—as if the less fruitful, the transient, the meaningless and worthless, the bad, the ugly and untrue and degrading were in any way more real than hope and trust in the good.

But the fact remains that the human being is the only entity known to us that, upon entering the world, expressed the hope that what is wrong and broken in the world can be healed. Of all the creatures known to us, it is only man who has faith, hope, and love. This in itself tells us a lot about our calling and it also tells us more about the inner and existential structure of human existence than we are sometimes prepared to admit: idealism, hope, a sense for value and meaning, and responsibility are part and parcel of our very nature.

This hope has always spurred human action. Only human beings see a deficit not only as a lamentable state of affairs, but also as an imperative, as a call to do something about it themselves: to alleviate suffering, to heal illnesses, to help the weak, and to be humane, not only human. This, in turn, is an important rebuke to the nihilist view, which does justice neither to our humanity (our hopes and our quest for meaning, compassion, connection, kindness, benevolence) nor to the world (its need for our hope and our will to meaning).

Our hope thus meets a world in need of healing. Indeed, the strongest voice of opposition to dogmatic nihilism is—in addition to our moral obligation and our conscious selves—the world itself, precisely in its broken state, its imperfection, and its need to be healed and made whole. For this brokenness tells us: the world, other people, our children, our parents, those in need, are dependent on us and our hope, and it is only man who carries this hope into the world at all. If he gives it up, it will disappear from the face of the Earth without a trace—with foreseeable consequences not only for the world, but also for the individual human being himself. The past century is largely a sad testimony of these consequences.

This means, however, that our hope is not a psychological deficiency or philosophical error; it is part of our nature, and therefore part also of this world. Rather, the psychological deficiency or philosophical error reveals itself in the rejection of our transcendent nature, our hope and meaning—for it is the rejection of a core characteristic of human experience of the self and the world (and of survival). And the error is the turning away from solace, art, truth-seeking, love, scientific discovery, compassion, connection, and the adventure of a meaningful and engaged life in the knowledge that this life is not just a fleeting flicker of the light of consciousness in what otherwise is dark and nonsentient nothingness.

When a candle burns down, wax dwindles down—just as our days dwindle down. But the wax isn't lost. It turns into light. Our journey through life on Earth, transitory as this life is, can turn into light, too—and yet, in contrast to the candle, this transformation doesn't happen automatically. Rather, we have the freedom and responsibility to choose to, and we may or may not turn our lives into light. And for the religious person there remains the additional hope that his light is salvaged in a greater light that carries and preserves everything, including himself, beyond illness, old age, and death.

As I have tried to show in this book, I think we have good reasons to believe that this hope can be justified. It stands on a secure foundation. Our analysis cannot go further than that, but at least it goes that far. And yet it is not only the hope that we ourselves will be preserved and protected and comforted, but also the hope that we will be protectors and comforters for others in our lifetime. We are all dependent on this, today more than ever: don't take away the soul. Rather: value it, nourish it, both others' and your own.

Acknowledgments

This book would never have become had not so many people entrusted me with their accounts of the death and dying of their loved ones, family members and friends, or patients. I thank them for sharing their memories with me. And I especially thank those who allowed me to include their accounts in this book. Some of these accounts I have translated from German or French into English, and some of my respondents were even kind enough to improve these translations to better reflect what they had experienced and witnessed. Thank you for sharing, and thank you for your trust.

Next, I want to thank my colleagues, students, and assistants both at the University of Vienna and at my Research Institute for Theoretical Psychology and Personalist Studies at Pázmány University in Budapest for their encouragement and insights, and I should also like to thank the audiences of my public lectures on terminal lucidity, especially at the Austrian Society for Border Areas of Psychology (Vienna, April 25, 2016), the Netzwerk Nahtoderfahrung in Freckenhorst, Westphalia (July 6, 2019), and at the Cognitive Science Fireside

Talks Conference in Düsseldorf (August 4, 2019), as well as the many members of the helping professions (nursing homes, hospices, hospitals). They have helped me sort out my ideas and explore questions in response to the needs and concerns of those directly affected and confronted with terminal lucidity and similar phenomena in their daily work. I thank them for their openness, their encouragement, and for the "homework" they entrusted to me. I sincerely hope that with this book I have at least partially lived up to this trust.

Much thanks go to Kenneth Ring, friend and colleague, and, in many ways, inspiration since my student days when I read his books but didn't yet know the wonderful, warm, and kind person behind them. Now this book—and more generally, my work on terminal lucidity—has connected us personally as well. I thank Ken for his critical review of the various versions of this book—and his valuable advice to completely rewrite its second part.

I would also like to thank George Witte, editor-in-chief at St. Martin's Press, for his interest in the subject, for his patience and for his unwavering belief in this project, and his careful reading and diligent editing of several versions of the manuscript, and my agent, Nat Sobel, for his support and kind advice.

So many people I should still thank. Among them Michael Nahm for his pioneering work on terminal lucidity, and for his help with the statistical evaluation of the initial analyses of the second pilot phase of the results of our questionnaire study described in part in chapter 8; and Georg-Philipp von Pezold for his translation work on the first draft of this book; and Basil Eldadah, Elena Fazio, and Kristina McLinden, all at the National Institute on Aging, for organizing and inviting me to the first Research Workshop on Paradoxical Lucidity at the NIA, which in many ways proved to be pathbreaking for the research discussed in this book.

I thank the editorial board of the *Journal for Near-Death Studies of the International Association for Near-Death Studies* (IANDS) for their kind permission to quote extensively from my article "Complex Visual Imagery and Cognition During Near-Death Experiences" (first published in the *Journal of Near-Death Studies*, issue 34:2, 2015) in chapter 12.

My foremost thanks go to my two daughters and especially to my wife, Juliane, for her patience, her support, and for the many wonderful conversations and ideas, many of which have gone into my research, and finally, into this book—and for so, so much more.

Bibliography

Aminoff, M. J., Scheinman, M. M., Griffin, J. C., & Herre, J. M. "Electrocerebral Accompaniments of Syncope Associated with Malignant Ventricular Arrhythmias." *Annals of Internal Medicine* 108 (1988): 791–796.

Bateson, M. C. *Composing a Life*. New York: Grove Press, 2001.

Batthyány, A. & Elitzur, A. (Eds.) *Irreducibly Conscious: Selected Papers on Consciousness.* Heidelberg: Universitätsverlag Winter.

Batthyány, A. & Greyson, B. "Spontaneous Remission of Dementia Before Death Results from a Study on Paradoxical Lucidity." *Psychology of Consciousness: Theory, Research, and Practice.* (2020).

Batthyány, A. "Complex Visual Imagery and Cognition During Near-Death Experiences." *Journal of Near-Death Studies* 34, no. 2 (2015): 65–83.

Batthyány, A. *Foundations of Near-Death Research: A Conceptual and Phenomenological Map*. Durham: IANDS Press, 2018.

Batthyány, A., & Elitzur, A. (Eds.) *Mind and Its Place in the World: Non-Reductionist Approaches to the Ontology of Consciousness*. De Gruyter, 2006.

Begley, S. "Of Voodoo and the Brain." *Newsweek,* VLIII, 25 (2009).

Bering, J. "One Last Goodbye: The Strange Case of Terminal Lucidity." *Scientific American*. November 25, 2014. https://blogs.scientificamerican.com/bering-in-mind/one -last-goodbye-the-strange-case-of-terminal-lucidity/.

Bloch, O. *Vom Tode*. Berlin: Juncker, 1903.

Blum, D. *Ghost Hunters: William James and the Search for Scientific Proof of Life after Death*. Penguin, 2007.

Brayne, S., Lovelace, H., & Fenwick, P. "End-of-life Experiences and the Dying Process in a Gloucestershire Nursing Home as Reported by Nurses and Care Assistants." *American Journal of Hospice and Palliative Medicine* 25, no. 3 (2008): 195–206.

Carruthers, G. "Confabulation or Experience? Implications of Out-of-Body Experiences for Theories of Consciousness. *Theory & Psychology*, 28, no. 1 (2018): 122–140.

Chalmers, D. *The Conscious Mind: In Search of a Fundamental Theory*. Oxford: Oxford University Press, 1996.

Cox-Chapman, M. *The Case for Heaven: Near-Death Experiences as Evidence of the Afterlife*. Putnam, 1995.

Crabtree, V. "Emotions Without Souls: How Biochemistry and Neurology Account for Feelings." (1996). Working paper.

Crick, F. *The Astonishing Hypothesis: The Scientific Search for the Soul*. New York: Simon and Schuster, 1994.

Cunningham, P. F. "Are Religious Experiences Really Localized Within the Brain? The Promise, Challenges, and Prospects of Neurotheology." *The Journal of Mind and Behavior* (2011): 223–249.

Dainton, B. *Stream of Consciousness: Unity and Continuity in Conscious Experience*. Routledge, 2002.

Dudukovic, N. M., Marsh, E. J., & Tversky, B. "Telling a Story or Telling It Straight: The Effects of Entertaining Versus Accurate Retellings on Memory." *Applied Cognitive Psychology* 18, no. 2 (2004): 125–143.

Eccles, J. C. *Facing Reality: Philosophical Adventures by a Brain Scientist*. New York: Springer, 2013.

Eccles, J. C. *The Human Psyche: The Gifford Lectures, University of Edinburgh 1978–1979*. New York: Springer, 2012.

Edwards, P. *Reincarnation: A Critical Investigation*. Buffalo: Prometheus Books, 2001.

Eldadah, B. A., Fazio, E. M., & McLinden, K. A. "Lucidity in Dementia: A Perspective from the NIA." *Alzheimer's & Dementia* 15, no. 8 (2019): 1104–1106.

Elitzur, A. C. "Consciousness Can No More Be Ignored." *Journal of Consciousness Studies* 2, no. 4 (1995): 353–357.

Elitzur, A. C. "Consciousness Makes a Difference: A Reluctant Dualist's Confession." In Batthyány, A., & Elitzur, A. C. (Eds.) *Irreducibly Conscious: Selected Papers on Consciousness*. Heidelberg: Universitätsverlag, 2009, 43–72.

Elitzur, A. C. "What's the Mind-Body Problem with You Anyway? Prolegomena to Any Scientific Discussion on Consciousness." In Batthyány, A., & Elitzur, A. C. (Eds.) *Mind and its Place in the World*. Frankfurt: Ontos, 2006, 15–22.

Ernst, E. (2002). A Systematic Review of Systematic Reviews of Homeopathy. *British Journal of Clinical Pharmacology* 54, no. 6 (2002): 577–582.

Fenwick, P., & Brayne, S. "End-of-Life Experiences: Reaching Out for Compassion, Communication, and Connection—Meaning of Deathbed Visions and Coincidences. *American Journal of Hospice and Palliative Medicine* 28 (2011): 7–15.

Fenwick, P., Lovelace, H., & Brayne, S. "Comfort for the Dying: Five-Year Retrospective and One-Year Prospective Studies of End of Life Experiences." *Archives of Gerontology and Geriatrics* 51, (2010): 173–179.

Fox, M. *Religion, Spirituality and the Near-Death Experience*. Routledge, 2003.

Frankl, V. E. *The Feeling of Meaninglessness: A Challenge to Psychotherapy and Philosophy*. Edited by Alexander Batthyány. Marquette University Press, 2010.

Frankl, V. E. *Man's Search for Meaning*. New York: Simon and Schuster, 1985.

Frankl, V. E. *Metaklinische Vorlesungen*. Wien: Viktor Frankl Archive, 1949.

Frankl, V. E. "The Spiritual Dimension in Existential Analysis and Logotherapy." *Journal of Individual Psychology* 15, no. 2 (1959): 157.

Frederick, S., Verduyn, P., Koval, P., et al. "The Relationship Between Arousal and the Remembered Duration of Positive Events." *Applied Cognitive Psychology* 27, no. 4 (2013): 493–496.

Gauld, A. *The Founders of Psychical Research*. Routledge, 2019.

Gendle, M. H. "Discussing Philosophy of Mind in Introductory Neuroscience Classes." *Journal of Undergraduate Neuroscience Education* 9, no. 2 (2011): E5.

Gibson, A. S. "Religious Wars or Healthy Competition in the NDE Movement?" *Journal of Near-Death Studies*, 18, no. 4 (2000): 273–276.

Greene, J. D. "Social Neuroscience and the Soul's Last Stand." *Social Neuroscience: Toward Understanding the Underpinnings of the Social Mind*. Oxford: Oxford University Press, 2011, 263–273.

Greyson, B. "Beyond the Mind-Body Problem: New Paradigms in the Science of Consciousness." Panel Discussion. United Nations, New York. September 11, 2008.

Greyson, B. *After: A Doctor Explores What Near-Death Experiences Reveal About Life and Beyond*. New York: Random House, 2021.

Greyson, B. "Implications of Near-Death Experiences for a Postmaterialist Psychology." *Psychology of Religion and Spirituality* 2 no. 1 (2010): 37.

Griffiths, P. (Ed.) *Philosophy, Psychology and Psychiatry*. Cambridge: Cambridge University Press, 1994.

Halford, H. *Essays and Orations, Read and Delivered at the Royal College of Physicians: To Which is Added an Account of the Opening of the Tomb of King Charles I*. London: John Murray, 1842.

Hodgson, D. "Neuroscience and Folk Psychology, an Overview." *Journal of Consciousness Studies* 1, no. 2 (1994): 205–216.

Holden, J. M. "Veridical Perception in Near-death Experiences." In J. M. Holden, B. Greyson, & D. James (Eds.) *The Handbook of Near-Death Experiences: Thirty Years of Investigation*. Praeger/ABC-CLIO, 2009, 185–211.

Hope, T. "Personal Identity and Psychiatric Illness." In Griffiths, P. (Ed.). *Philosophy, Psychology and Psychiatry*. Cambridge: Cambridge University Press, 1994.

Huxley, A. *The Doors of Perception: And Heaven and Hell*. London: Chatto and Windus, 1954.

Jackson, F. "Epiphenomenal Qualia." *Philosophical Quarterly* 32 (1982): 127–136.

James, W. "Address of the President Before the Society for Psychical Research." *Science* 3, no. 77 (1896): 881–888.

James, W. "Subjective Effects of Nitrous Oxide." In James, W. *Collected Essays and Reviews*. London: Longmans, Green and Company, 1896.

Jenner, E. (1801). "On the Origin of the Vaccine Inoculation." *The Medical and Physical journal* 5, no. 28 (1801): 505.

Jünger E. *The Storm of Steel: From the Diary of a German Storm-Troop Officer on the Western Front*. London: Chatto and Windus, 1996.

Karamanou, M., Liappas, I., Ch, A., Androutsos, G., & Lykouras, E. "Julius Wagner-Jauregg (1857–1940): Introducing Fever Therapy in the Treatment of Neurosyphilis." *Psychiatrike Psychiatriki* 24, no. 3 (2013): 208–212.

Kelly, E. W., Greyson, B., & Kelly, E. F. "Unusual Experiences near Death and Related Phenomena." In E. F. Kelly, E. W. Kelly, A. Crabtree, A. Gauld, M. Grosso, & B. Greyson, *Irreducible Mind*. Lanham, MD: Rowman & Littlefield, 2007.

Kelly, E. W., Greyson, B., & Stevenson, I. "Can Experiences near Death Furnish Evidence of Life After Death?" *OMEGA—Journal of Death and Dying* 40, no. 4 (2000): 513–519.

Koriat, A., & Levy-Sadot, R. "Processes Underlying Metacognitive Judgments: Information-Based and Experience-Based Monitoring of One's Own Knowledge." In: S. Chaiken & Y. Trope (Eds.), Dual-Process Theories in Social Psychology. New York: The Guildford Press (pp. 483–502).(1999)

Kübler-Ross, E. Leben und Sterben: Ein Vortrag (Tape). Telfs: Audiotex, 1989

Lehrer, J. *The Decisive Moment: How the Brain Makes up its Mind*. Canongate Books, 2009, 102–104.

Leubuscher, R. "Wiederkehr des Bewußteins vor dem Tode einer Blödsinnigen." *Medicinische Zeitung von dem Verein für Heilkunde in Preussen* (1848): 48.

Lim, C. Y., Park, J. Y., Kim, D. Y., Yoo, K. D., Kim, H. J., Kim, Y., & Shin, S. J. "Terminal Lucidity in the Teaching Hospital Setting." *Death Studies* 44, no. 5 (2018): 285–291.

Lindley D. "Response to Robert Lanza." *USA Today*. http://www.usatoday.com/tech/science/2007–03–09-lanza-response_N.htm. Accessed Nov 21, 2020.

Löhr, J. *Über das Wiedererwachen des Bewusstseins kurz vor dem Tode der Irren,* 1848.

Lukas, E. *Rat in ratloser Zeit*. Freiburg: Herder, 1988.

Macleod, AD. "Lightening Up Before Death." *Palliative & Supportive Care* 7, no. 4: 516.

Martens, P. R. "Near-Death Experiences in Out-of-Hospital Cardiac Arrest Survivors. Meaningful Phenomena or Just Fantasy of Death?" *Resuscitation* 27, no. 2 (1994): 171–175.

Mashour, G.A., Frank, L., Batthyány, A., et al. "Paradoxical Lucidity: A Potential Paradigm Shift for the Neurobiology and Treatment of Severe Dementias." *Alzheimer's and Dementia* 15 (2019): 1107–1114. Mast, B. T. *Second Forgetting: Remembering the Power of the Gospel during Alzheimer's Disease*. Zondervan, 2014.

Mays, R. G., & Mays, S. B. "Explaining near-death experiences: Physical or non-physical causation?" *Journal of Near-Death Studies* 33, no. 3 (2015): 125–149.

Mays, R. G., & Mays, S. B. "Near-death experiences: Extended naturalism or promissory physicalism? A response to Fischer's article." *Journal of Consciousness Studies* 27, nos. 11–12 (2020): 222–236.

Medawar, P. B. & Jean S. *The Life Science: Current Ideas of Biology*. New York: HarperCollins Publishers, 1997.

Moody, R. A. *Life After Life*. Mockingbird Books, 1975.

Munk, William. *Euthanasia: Or Medical Treatment in Aid of an Easy Death*. London: Longmans, Green and Co., 1887, 34–37.

Nahm, M. "Terminal Lucidity in People with Mental Illness and Other Mental Disability: An Overview and Implications for Possible Explanatory Models." *Journal of Near-Death Studies* 28, no. 2 (2009): 87.

Nahm, M. "Wenn die Dunkelheit ein Ende findet." *Terminale Geistesklarheit und andere Phanomene in Todesnähe*. Amerang: Crotona, 2012.

Nahm, M., & Greyson, B. "The Death of Anna Katharina Ehmer: A Case Study in Terminal Lucidity." *OMEGA—Journal of Death and Dying* 68, no. 1 (2014): 77–87.

Nahm, M., & Greyson, B. "Terminal Lucidity in Patients with Chronic Schizophrenia and Dementia: A Survey of the Literature." *The Journal of Nervous and Mental Disease* 197, no. 12 (2009): 942–944.

Nahm, M., Greyson B., Kelly, E. W., and Haraldsson, E., "Terminal Lucidity: A Review and a Case Collection." *Archives of Gerontology and Geriatrics* 55 (2012): 138–142.

Noyes Jr., R., & Kletti, R. "Depersonalization in the Face of Life-Threatening Danger: A Description." *Psychiatry* 39, no. 1 (1976): 19–27.

Noyes Jr, R., & Kletti, R. "Depersonalization in the Face of Life-Threatening Danger: An Interpretation." *OMEGA—Journal of Death and Dying* 7, no. 2 (1976): 103–114.

Owens, J. E., Cook, E. W., & Stevenson, I. "Features of 'Near-Death Experience' in Relation to Whether or Not Patients Were near Death." *The Lancet* 336 (1990): 1175–1177.

Parnia, S., Waller, D. G., Yeates, R., & Fenwick, P. "A Qualitative and Quantitative Study of the Incidence, Features and Aetiology of Near-death Experiences in Cardiac Arrest Survivors." *Resuscitation* 48, no. 2 (2001), 149–156.

Plato. *Plato in Twelve Volumes, Vol. 1.* trans. Harold North Fowler. Cambridge, MA: Harvard University Press, 1966.

Popper, K. & Eccles, J.C. *The Self and Its Brain. An Argument for Interactionism.* New York: Springer, 1977.

Provine, W. (ca. 1995). W. Provine (ca. 1995). Transcript of a public lecture given ca. 1995.

Ring, K. "Miraculous Returns: Terminal Lucidity and the Work of Alexander Batthyány." *Notes from the Ringdom*. February 2022.

Ring, K. "Religious Wars in the NDE Movement: Some Personal Reflections on Michael Sabom's Light & Death." *Journal of Near-Death Studies* 18, no. 4 (2000): 215–244.

Ring, K., & Cooper, S. *Mindsight: Near-death and Out-of-body Experiences in the Blind.* iUniverse, 2008.

Ring, K., & Cooper, S. "Near-death and Out-of-body Experiences in the Blind: A Study of Apparent Eyeless Vision." *Journal of Near-Death Studies* 16, no. 2 (1997): 101–147.

Sabom, M. "Response to Kenneth Ring's 'Religious Wars in the NDE Movement: Some Personal Reflections on Michael Sabom's *Light & Death.*'" *Journal of Near-Death Studies* 18, no. 4 (2000): 245–271.

Sabom, M. "The Shadow of Death." *Christian Research Journal* 26, no. 2 (2003).

Sabom, M. B. "The Near-Death Experience: Myth or Reality? A Methodological Approach." *Anabiosis: The Journal of Near-Death Studies* 1 (1981): 44–56.

Sabom, M. B. *Recollections of Death: A Medical Investigation.* New York, NY: Harper and Row, 1982, 111–113.

Sanders, M. A. *Nearing Death Awareness: A Guide to the Language, Visions, and Dreams of the Dying.* Jessica Kingsley Publishers, 2007.

Sartori, P. *The Near-Death Experiences of Hospitalized Intensive Care Patients: A Five-year Clinical Study.* Lewiston: Edward Mellen Press, 2008.

Savva, Louie. "Open Letter to Susan Blackmore," 2006.

Searle, J. R. *Wiederentdeckung des Geistes.* Artemis & Winkler, 1994.

Sherrington, C. S. *Man on His Nature.* Cambridge: Cambridge University Press, 1951.

Simmons, E. J. *Pushkin.* London: Oxford University Press, 1937.

Smart, J. C. "Religion and Science." In *The Encyclopedia of Philosophy* vol. 7. New York, 1980.

Smith, K. A. "Edward Jenner and the Smallpox Vaccine." *Frontiers in Immunology* 2, no. 21 (2011).

Spaemann, R. *Personen: Versuche über den Unterschied zwischen "etwas" und "jemand."* Stuttgart: Klett-Cotta, 1996.

Stark, F. M. *Perseus in the Wind.* London: Cox & Wyman Ltd., 1948.

Swinburne, R. "Interview on Mind-Body-Dualism." *Science and Religion News,* 2006.

Swinburne, R. *Is There a God?* Oxford University Press, 2010.

Tobias, S., & Everson, H. T. "Studying the Relationship Between Affective and Metacognitive Variables." *Anxiety, Stress, and Coping* 10, no. 1 (1997): 59–81.

Tomberg, Valentin *The Art of the Good: On the Regeneration of Fallen Justice*. New York: Angelico Press, 2021.

Turetskaia, B. E. & Romanenko, A. A. "Predsmertnye remissii v konechnykh sostoianiiakh shizofrenii [Agonal remission in the terminal stages of schizophrenia]." *Journal of Neuropathology and Psychiatry* 75 (1975): 559–562.

Van Lommel, P. *Consciousness Beyond Life*. New York: HarperCollins, 2010.

Van Lommel, P., Van Wees, R., Meyers, V., & Elfferich, I. *Near-Death Experience in Survivors of Cardiac Arrest: A Prospective Study in the Netherlands*. Routledge, 2017, 91–97.

Vik-Mo, A. O., Giil, L. M., Borda, M. G., Ballard, C., & Aarsland, D. "The Individual Course of Neuropsychiatric Symptoms in People with Alzheimer's and Lewy Body Dementia: 12-Year Longitudinal Cohort Study." *The British Journal of Psychiatry* 216, no. 1 (2020): 43–48.

Whitrow, M. "Wagner-Jauregg and Fever Therapy." *Medical History* 34, no. 3 (1990): 294–310.

Wittneben, W. "Erziehung, Behandlung und Pflege Geistesschwacher. " *Geisteskrankenpflege* (1934): 38.

Wooten-Green, R. *When the Dying Speak: How to Listen to and Learn from Those Facing Death*. Chicago: Loyola, 2001.

Zaleski, C. *Otherworld Journeys: Accounts of Near-Death Experience in Medieval and Modern times*. Oxford: Oxford University Press, 1988.

Notes

1: ON BEING SOMEONE, AND YET TO DIE

1. G. A. Mashour, L. Frank, A. Batthyány, et al., "Paradoxical Lucidity: A Potential Paradigm Shift for the Neurobiology and Treatment of Severe Dementias," *Alzheimer's and Dementia* 15 (2019): 1107–1114.
2. K. Ring, "Miraculous Returns: Terminal Lucidity and the Work of Alexander Batthyány," *Notes from the Ringdom* (February 2022).
3. B. Greyson, *After: A Doctor Explores What Near-Death Experiences Reveal About Life and Beyond* (New York: Random House, 2021).
4. It was Michael Nahm who coined the term *terminal lucidity*. Otherwise, the phenomenon is sometimes referred to as "the final goodbye," "the last hurrah," or the "end of life rally."
5. P. B. Medawar & Jean S. Medawar, *The Life Science: Current Ideas of Biology* (New York: HarperCollins Publishers, 1977), 22.
6. C. S. Sherrington, *Man on His Nature* (Cambridge: Cambridge University Press, 1951), 92

2: DEATH, DISEASE, AND THE QUESTION OF WHO WE ARE

1. B. T. Mast, *Second Forgetting: Remembering the Power of the Gospel During Alzheimer's Disease* (Zondervan: 2014), 9.
2. F. M. Stark, *Perseus in the Wind*. (London: Cox & Wyman Ltd., 1948), 158
3. Plato, *Plato in Twelve Volumes, Vol. 1, trans. Harold North Fowler* (Cambridge, MA: Harvard University Press, 1966).
4. Ibid.

5.   S. Begley, "Of Voodoo and the Brain," *Newsweek VLIII*, no 25 (2009).

6.   Valentin Tomberg, *The Art of the Good: On the Regeneration of Fallen Justice* (New York: Angelico Press, 2021).

7.   D. Hodgson (1994). "Neuroscience and Folk Psychology, an Overview," *Journal of Consciousness Studies* 1, no. 2 (1994): 205–216.

8.   K. R. Popper and J. C. Eccles, *The Self and Its Brain* (New York/Berlin: Springer, 1977).

9.   J. C. Eccles, *How the Self Controls Its Brain* (New York: Springer, 1994).

10. J. Lehrer, *The Decisive Moment: How the Brain Makes up Its Mind* (Canongate Books, 2009), 102–104.

11. J. J. C. Smart, "Religion and Science," in *The Encyclopedia of Philosophy* vol. 7 (New York: Academia, 1980), S.161.

12. P. Edwards, *Reincarnation: A Critical Investigation* (Buffalo, NY: Prometheus Books, 2001), 286.

13. V. Crabtree, *Emotions Without Souls: How Biochemistry and Neurology Account for Feelings,* working paper (1999).

14. F. Crick, *The Astonishing Hypothesis: The Scientific Search for the Soul* (New York: Simon and Schuster, 1994), S.1f.

15. W. Provine (ca. 1995). Transcript of a public lecture given ca. 1995.

16. Louie Savva, Open letter to Susan Blackmore (2006). The open letter is no longer available on Savva's website EverythingIsPointless.com, but can be accessed at https://web.archive.org/web/20110923061215/http://www.everythingispointless.com/2006/11/conversation-with-susan-blackmore.html

3: THE RETURN OF THE SELF

1.   M. Nahm, Wenn die Dunkelheit ein Ende findet, *Terminale Geistesklarheit und andere Phanomene in Todesnähe* (Amerang: Crotona, 2012); M. Nahm et al, "Terminal Lucidity: A Review and a Case Collection," *Archives of Gerontology and Geriatrics* 55, no. 1 (2012): 138–142; M. Nahm, "Terminal Lucidity in People with Mental Illness and Other Mental Disability: An Overview and Implications for Possible Explanatory Models," *Journal of Near-Death Studies* 28, no. 2 (2009): 87.

2.   O. Bloch (1903). *Vom Tode* (Berlin: Juncker, 1903), 545f.; as cited in M. Nahm, Wenn die Dunkelheit ein Ende findet, *Terminale Geistesklarheit und andere Phanomene in Todesnähe* (Amerang: Crotona, 2012), 13.

3.   G. A. Mashour, L. Frank, A. Batthyány, et al. (2019), "Paradoxical Lucidity: A Potential Paradigm Shift for the Neurobiology and Treatment of Severe Dementias," *Alzheimer's and Dementia* 15 (2019): 1107–1114.

4.   M. Nahm, Wenn die Dunkelheit ein Ende findet, *Terminale Geistesklarheit und andere Phanomene in Todesnähe* (Amerang: Crotona, 2012), 35.

5.   As cited in J. Löhr, "Über das Wiedererwachen des Bewusstseins kurz vor dem Tode der Irren," *Zeitschrift für die Staatsarzneikunde* 55 (1848): p. 266f.

6.   R. Leubuscher, "Wiederkehr des Bewußtseins vor dem Tode einer Blödsinnigen," *Medicinische Zeitung von dem Verein für Heilkunde in Preussen* 48 (1848): 227; as cited in M. Nahm, Wenn die Dunkelheit ein Ende findet, *Terminale Geistesklarheit und andere Phanomene in Todesnähe* (Amerang: Crotona, 2012), 36.

7.   R. Leubuscher, "Wiederkehr des Bewußtseins vor dem Tode einer Blödsinnigen," *Medicinische Zeitung von dem Verein für Heilkunde in Preussen* 48 (1848): 228; as

cited in M. Nahm, Wenn die Dunkelheit ein Ende findet, *Terminale Geistesklarheit und andere Phanomene in Todesnähe* (Amerang: Crotona, 2012), 36.

8. M. Nahm and B. Greyson, "The Death of Anna Katharina Ehmer: A Case Study in Terminal Lucidity," *OMEGA—Journal of Death and Dying* 68, no. 1 (2014): 77–87.

9. M. Nahm, Wenn die Dunkelheit ein Ende findet, *Terminale Geistesklarheit und andere Phanomene in Todesnähe* (Amerang: Crotona, 2012), 61.

10. W. Wittneben, Erziehung, Behandlung und Pflege Geistesschwacher. *Geisteskrankenpflege* 38 (1934): 153; as cited in M. Nahm, Wenn die Dunkelheit ein Ende findet, *Terminale Geistesklarheit und andere Phanomene in Todesnähe* (Amerang: Crotona, 2012), 63.

11. Ibid.

12. M. Nahm and B. Greyson, "Terminal Lucidity in Patients with Chronic Schizophrenia and Dementia: A Survey of the Literature," *The Journal of Nervous and Mental disease* 197, no. 12 (2009): 942–944; M. Nahm, "Terminal Lucidity in People with Mental Illness and Other Mental Disability: An Overview and Implications for Possible Explanatory Models," *Journal of Near-Death Studies* 28, no. 2 (2009): 87.

13. A. S. Macleod, "Lightening Up Before Death," *Palliative & Supportive Care* 7, no. 4 (2009): 513.

14. E. J. Simmons, *Pushkin* (London: Oxford University Press, 1937), 422; Ibid.

15. M. Nahm et al, "Terminal Lucidity: A Review and a Case Collection," *Archives of Gerontology and Geriatrics* 55 (2012): 138–142.

16. S. Brayne, H. Lovelace, and P. Fenwick, "End-of-Life Experiences and the Dying Process in a Gloucestershire Nursing Home as Reported by Nurses and Care Assistants," *American Journal of Hospice and Palliative Medicine* 25, no. 3 (2008): 195–206.

17. A. S. Macleod, "Lightening Up Before Death," *Palliative & Supportive Care* 7, no. 4 (2009): 513–516.

4: SETTING THE SCENE

1. E. Jenner, "On the Origin of the Vaccine Inoculation," *The Medical and Physical Journal* 5, no. 28 (1801): 505; K. A. Smith, "Edward Jenner and the Smallpox Vaccine," *Frontiers in Immunology* 2, no. 21 (2011).

2. J. Bering, "One Last Goodbye: The Strange Case of Terminal Lucidity," *Scientific American* blog (November 2014). Available from: https://blogs.scientificamerican.com/bering-in–mind/one-last-goodbye-thestrange-case-of-terminal-lucidity/ [Accessed on August 1, 2020].

3. V. E. Frankl, *The Feeling of Meaninglessness: A Challenge to Psychotherapy and Philosophy*, ed. Alexander Batthyány (Marquette University Press); V. E. Frankl, "The Spiritual Dimension in Existential Analysis and Logotherapy," *Journal of Individual Psychology* 15, no. 2 (1959), 157.

4. V. E. Frankl, *Metaklinische Vorlesungen* (Wien: Viktor Frankl Archive, 1949).

5. E. Kübler-Ross, Leben und Sterben: Ein Vortrag (Tape). Telfs: Audiotex, 1989

6. A. S. Macleod, "Lightening Up before Death," *Palliative & Supportive Care* 7, no. 4 (2009): 513–516.

5: APPROACHING TERMINAL LUCIDITY: THE PILOT STUDY
AND ITS AFTERMATH

1.   Mays, R. G., & Mays, S. B. "Explaining Near-Death Experiences: Physical or Non-physical Causation?" *Journal of Near-Death Studies* 33, no. 3, (2015): 125–149; Mays, R. G., & Mays, S. B. "Near-Death Experiences: Extended Naturalism or Promissory Physicalism? A Response to Fischer's Article." *Journal of Consciousness Studies* 27 nos. 11–12, (2020): 222–236.
2.   A. Batthyány, *Foundations of Near-Death Research: A Conceptual and Phenomenological Map* (Durham: IANDS Press, 2018).

6: "WE NEED TO TALK": THE LONELINESS OF WITNESSING
THE UNEXPECTED

1.   R. A. Moody, *Life After Life* (Mockingbird Books, 1975).
2.   S. Parnia et al., "A Qualitative and Quantitative Study of the Incidence, Features and Aetiology of Near-Death Experiences in Cardiac Arrest Survivors," *Resuscitation* 48, no. 2 (2001): 149–156; P. Van Lommel et al. *Near-Death Experience in Survivors of Cardiac Arrest: A Prospective Study in the Netherlands* (Routledge, 2017), 91–97.
3.   C. Zaleski, *Otherworld Journeys: Accounts of Near-Death Experience in Medieval and Modern Times* (Oxford University Press, 1988); M. Fox, *Religion, Spirituality and the Near-Death Experience* (Routledge, 2003).
4.   R. Wooten-Green, *When the Dying Speak: How to Listen to and Learn from Those Facing Death* (Chicago: Loyola, 2001), 119. I owe the reference to this case and Wooten-Green's excellent book to Michael Nahm, who cites it in his book.

7: CASTING OUT THE NETS

1.   A. Batthyány and B. Greyson, "Spontaneous Remission of Dementia Before Death: Results from a Study on Paradoxical Lucidity," *Psychology of Consciousness: Theory, Research, and Practice* (2020).
2.   G. A. Mashour, L. Frank, A. Batthyány, et al., "Paradoxical Lucidity: A Potential Paradigm Shift for the Neurobiology and Treatment of Severe Dementias," *Alzheimer's and Dementia* 15, no. 8 (2019): 1107–1114.
3.   C. Y. Lim et al., "Terminal Lucidity in the Teaching Hospital Setting," *Death Studies* 44, no. 5 (2018): 285–291.

8: WITNESSES

1.   A. O. Vik-Mo, et al., "The Individual Course of Neuropsychiatric Symptoms in People with Alzheimer's and Lewy Body Dementia: 12-Year Longitudinal Cohort Study," *The British Journal of Psychiatry* 216, no. 1 (2020), 43–48.
2.   B. E. Turetskaia and A. A. Romanenko,"Predsmertnye remissii v konechnykh sostoianiiakh shizofrenii [Agonal remission in the terminal stages of schizophrenia]," *Journal of Neuropathology and Psychiatry* 75 (1975): 559–562.
3.   P. Fenwick and S. Brayne, "End-of-Life Experiences: Reaching Out for Compassion, Communication, and Connection—Meaning of Deathbed Visions and

Coincidences," *American Journal of Hospice and Palliative Medicine* 28 (2011): 7–15; P. Fenwick, H. Lovelace, and S. Brayne, "Comfort for the Dying: Five-Year Retrospective and One-Year Prospective Studies of End-of-Life Experiences," *Archives of Gerontology and Geriatrics* 51 (2010): 173–179.

4.   I owe this reference to Ron Wooten-Green whose book *When the Dying Speak* I wholeheartedly recommend to anyone interested in how to communicate with and especially how to listen to and learn from the dying.

5.   M. A. Sanders, *Nearing Death Awareness: A Guide to the Language, Visions, and Dreams of the Dying* (Jessica Kingsley Publishers, 2007), 27.

6.   A. S. Macleod, "Lightening Up Before Death," *Palliative & Supportive Care* 7, no. 4 (2009): 516.

7.   P. Fenwick and S. Brayne, "End-of-Life Experiences: Reaching Out for Compassion, Communication, and Connection—Meaning of Deathbed Visions and Coincidences," *American Journal of Hospice and Palliative Medicine* 28 (2011): 7–15.

9: WHITE CROWS

1.   B. A. Eldadah, E. M. Fazio, and K. A. McLinden, "Lucidity in Dementia: A Perspective from the NIA," *Alzheimer's & Dementia* 15, no. 8 (2019): 1104–1106.

2.   William Munk, *Euthanasia: or Medical Treatment in Aid of an Easy Death* (London: Longmans, Green and Co., 1887), 34–37.

3.   Happich 1932, cited in: M. Trost (1983). Friedrich Happich. Self-published booklet; English translation in M. Nahm & B. Greyson, "The Death of Anna Katharina Ehmer: A Case Study in Terminal Lucidity." *OMEGA—Journal of Death and Dying* 68, no. 1 (2014): 77–87.

4.   W. James, "Address of the President Before the Society for Psychical Research," *Science* 3, no. 77 (1896): 881–888.

5.   P. F. Cunningham, "Are Religious Experiences Really Localized within the Brain? The Promises, Challenges, and Prospects of Neurotheology," *The Journal of Mind and Behavior* (2011): 223–249.

10: MIND AND BRAIN IN EXTREME STATES

1.   G. A. Mashour, L. Frank, A. Batthyány, et al. (2019), "Paradoxical Lucidity: A Potential Paradigm Shift for the Neurobiology and Treatment of Severe Dementias," *Alzheimer's and Dementia* 15 (2019): 1107–1114.

2.   B. Greyson, Panel Discussion, "Beyond the Mind-Body Problem: New Paradigms in the Science of Consciousness," United Nations, New York (September 11, 2008).

11: MIND AT DEATH

1.   K. Ring and S. Cooper, "Near-Death and Out-of-Body Experiences in the Blind: A Study of Apparent Eyeless Vision," *Journal of Near-Death Studies* 16, no. 2 (1997): 101–147; K. Ring and S. Cooper, *Mindsight: Near-Death and Out-of-Body Experiences in the Blind* (iUniverse, 2008).

2.   M. Nahm, Wenn die Dunkelheit ein Ende findet, *Terminale Geistesklarheit und andere Phänomene in Todesnähe* (Amerang: Crotona, 2012), 184.

3.   R. Noyes Jr. and R. Kletti (1976). "Depersonalization in the Face of Life-Threatening Danger: A Description," *Psychiatry* 39, no. 1 (1976), 19–27; R. Noyes Jr. and R. Kletti, "Depersonalization in the Face of Life-Threatening Danger: An Interpretation," *OMEGA—Journal of Death and Dying* 7, no. 2 (1976), 103–114; G. Carruthers, "Confabulation or Experience? Implications of Out-of-Body Experiences for Theories of Consciousness," *Theory & Psychology* 28, no. 1 (2018), 122–140; P. R. Martens, "Near-Death Experiences in Out-of-Hospital Cardiac Arrest Survivors: Meaningful Phenomena or Just Fantasy of Death?," *Resuscitation* 27, no. 2 (1994), 171–175.

4.   Cf. M. Cox-Chapman, *The Case for Heaven: Near-Death Experiences as Evidence of the Afterlife* (Putnam, 1995).

12: PERCEPTION AT THE END OF LIFE

1.   B. Greyson, "Implications of Near-Death Experiences for a Post-materialist Psychology," *Psychology of Religion and Spirituality* 2 (2010): 37–45.

2.   B. Greyson, "Implications of Near-death Experiences for a Post-materialist Psychology," *Psychology of Religion and Spirituality* 2 (2010): 37.

3.   M. Sabom, "The Shadow of Death," *Christian Research Journal* 26, no. 2 (2003); see also M. Sabom, "The Near-Death Experience: Myth or Reality? A Methodological Approach," *Anabiosis: The Journal of Near-Death Studies* 1 (1981), 44–56.

4.   Ibid.

5.   M. Sabom, *Recollections of Death: A Medical Investigation* (New York: Harper and Row, 1982), 111–113.

6.   P. Sartori, *The Near-Death Experiences of Hospitalized Intensive Care Patients: A Five-year Clinical Study* (Lewiston: Edward Mellen Press, 2008).

7.   E. W. Kelly, B. Greyson, and I. Stevenson, "Can Experiences Near Death Furnish Evidence of Life After Death?" *OMEGA—Journal of Death and Dying* 40, no. 4 (2000): 513–519.

8.   J. M. Holden, "Veridical Perception in Near-Death Experiences," in J. M. Holden, B. Greyson, & D. James (eds.), *The Handbook of Near-Death Experiences: Thirty Years of Investigation* (2009), 185–211.

9.   N. M. Dudukovic, E. J. Marsh, and B. Tversky, "Telling a Story or Telling it Straight: The Effects of Entertaining Versus Accurate Retellings on Memory," *Applied Cognitive Psychology* 18, no. 2 (2004), 125–143.

10. K. Ring, "Religious Wars in the NDE Movement: Some Personal Reflections on Michael Sabom's *Light & Death*," *Journal of Near-Death Studies* 18, no. 4 (2000), 215–244; A. S. Gibson, "Religious Wars or Healthy Competition in the NDE Movement?," *Journal of Near-Death Studies* 18, no. 4 (2000), 273–276; M. Sabom, "Response to Kenneth Ring's 'Religious Wars in the NDE Movement: Some Personal Reflections on Michael Sabom's *Light & Death*.'" *Journal of Near-Death Studies* 18, no. 4 (2000), 245–271.

11. E. W. Kelly, B. Greyson, and E. F. Kelly, "Unusual Experiences Near Death and Related Phenomena," in E. F. Kelly et al, *Irreducible Mind* (Lanham, MD: Rowman & Littlefield, 2007), 386.

12. J. E. Owens, E. W. Cook, and I. Stevenson, "Features of 'Near-Death Experience' in Relation to Whether or not Patients Were Near Death," *The Lancet* (1990), 336, 1175–1177.

13: MIND, MEMORY, AND VISION NEAR DEATH

1. A. Batthyány, "Complex Visual Imagery and Cognition During Near-Death Experiences," *Journal of Near-Death Studies* 34, no. 2 (2015), 65–83.

14: RELATING THE NDE AND TL

1. S. Tobias and H. T. Everson, "Studying the Relationship Between Affective and Metacognitive Variables," *Anxiety, Stress, and Coping* 10, no. 1 (1997), 59–81; A. Koriat and R. Levy-Sadot, "Processes Underlying Metacognitive Judgments: Information-Based and Experience-Based Monitoring of One's Own Knowledge," In: S. Chaiken & Y. Trope (Eds.), *Dual-Process Theories in Social Psychologe*. New York: The Guildford Press (pp. 483–502).(1999).
2. W. James, "Subjective Effects of Nitrous Oxide," *Collected Essays and Reviews* (London: Longmans, Green and Company, 1920).
3. Ibid.

15: MAKING SENSE OF IT

1. Elitzur, A. C. "Consciousness Can No More Be Ignored." *Journal of Consciousness Studies* 2, no. 4 (1995): 353–357.
2. A. Huxley, *The Doors of Perception: And Heaven and Hell* (London: Chatto and Windus, 1954).
3. Some colleagues, such as Richard Swinburne (Univ. of Oxford), John C. Eccles (Univ. of Oxford and Melbourne), John Beloff (Edinburgh Univ.), Charles Taliaferro (St. Olaf College), Daniel N. Robinson (Univ. of Georgetown), William Hasker (Edinburgh Univ.), Uwe Meixner (Regensburg Univ.), Geoffrey Madell (Edinburgh Univ.), John Foster (Univ. of Oxford), Mark C. Baker (Rutgers Univ.), Stewart Goetz (Ursinus College), Dean Zimmermann (Rutgers Univ.), and others have been or are working on elaborated dualist or otherwise non-materialist theories of the conscious mind, and I would like to direct interested readers to these authors.

16: A SHELTERED SELF

1. J. C. Eccles, *The Human Psyche: The Gifford Lectures, University of Edinburgh 1978–1979* (New York: Springer Science, 2012).

17: WHY IT MATTERS

1. V. E. Frankl, *Man's Search for Meaning* (New York: Simon and Schuster, 1985).
2. Louie Savva, Open letter to Susan Blackmore (2006). The open letter is no longer available on Savva's website EverythingIsPointless.com, but can be accessed at https: //web.archive.org/web/20110923061215/http://www.everythingispointless.com/2006/11/conversation-with-susan-blackmore.html
3. D. Lindley, "Response to Robert Lanza," available at: http://www.usatoday.com/tech/science/2007–03–09-lanza-response_N.htm. Accessed Nov 21, 2020.

Index